21st Century Revenge
Down and Dirty Tactics for the Millennium

21st Century Revenge
Down and Dirty Tactics for the Millennium

by Victor Santoro

Loompanics Unlimited
Port Townsend, Washington

This book is sold for informational purposes only. Neither the author nor the publisher will be held accountable for the use or misuse of the information contained in this book.

21st Century Revenge: Down and Dirty Tactics for the Millennium

Published by:
Loompanics Unlimited
PO Box 1197
Port Townsend, WA 98368

Cover artwork by Jim Blanchard

ISBN 1-55950-191-X
Library of Congress Card Catalog 99-60179

Contents

Introduction

It's been two decades since the first revenge book, my *Techniques of Harassment*, (Desert Publications, 1979), appeared. During that time, our world has changed drastically, in some ways for the better, and in other ways for the worse. Regarding techniques of harassment and revenge, there's both good news and bad news. As the astute student of harassment has discovered, the bad news is that some techniques that were perfectly workable twenty years ago will not work today, and will in fact expose the person who tries them to counter-harassment, prosecution, or other retaliation. Some tried and true techniques still work very well, and perhaps better than ever. We'll explore these in due course.

One device that has radically changed the nature of harassment techniques is Caller ID. Today, when you make a telephone call, your name and number appear on a screen next to the telephone you're calling. In fact, some recent models have a Caller ID display right on the telephone itself. This means you can no longer telephone a pizza shop and have a dozen pies delivered to your target. You cannot place a classified ad in a newspaper to sell your target's house by telephone anymore, unless you have direct access to your target's phone. If so, you can exploit Caller ID to cause your target many problems that will bite him harder precisely because they are linked to his telephone. You can also subscribe to "blocked call" service, which means that your number and identity will not appear on the recipient's screen. Instead, a "Private Call" line will appear. This is, however, a warning to the person called that the caller is operating anonymously, and this can stall your plan. Another point to note about blocked call service is that it does not work when calling 911 or some other government agencies. Not only do your name and number show on the dispatcher's console, but also your address and other pertinent information.

The good news is that social changes have provided new or enhanced opportunities for harassment. The rise of "political correctness" allows you to make your target's life miserable by turning employers, fellow employees, and neighbors against him. We'll devote an entire chapter to this new development.

Another social change is bad news: the increasingly pervasive and aggressive commercialism that plagues our society. Today, we are bombarded with advertisements on radio and TV, while our privacy is invaded by telemarketers, who call us at home at inconvenient times. Commercial advertisers flood our mailboxes with junk mail, some of which is printed to resemble checks, to entice us to open and read it. The good news is that there are effective ways of fighting back, of treating them as aggressively as they treat us, and we'll cover these in detail in the appropriate chapters.

More bad news is that we're under more pressure today. Jobs are not as secure as they were two decades ago, and many have discovered that good work and loyalty don't count for beans when "downsizing" time arrives. The plethora of mergers, acquisitions, and hostile takeovers has resulted in many faithful and competent employees losing their jobs as victims of company politics. Among the frightened survivors there are some predatory types who curry favor with the boss to preserve their jobs. These are the company spies, the brown-nosers, the gossips, and the politickers who try to tear down other employees to safeguard their own employment. Today there is great concern over workplace violence, because employees who are being victimized by vicious supervisors sometimes *do* "go postal," and retaliate with gunfire against their tormentors.

If you're the victim of one of these poisonous predators, the thought of revenge has surely crossed your mind. Take heart: There is something you can do, and it doesn't have to be violent. It doesn't have to land you in more trouble than you're already suffering.

The growth of the Internet is good news for the revenge artist. This is both a significant new source of information and a vehicle to cause your target severe problems, even if he's not on the Net himself. There are Web sites listing the latest techniques for harassment and revenge, and forums for exchanging revenge information.

There is more good news, owing to new techniques such as "gaslighting," as explained in the book of the same title.[1] This is a program of psychological tactics and pressure to destroy your target's self-confidence and slowly drive him crazy. Combined with more conventional harassment methods, gaslighting can make your target's life unbearable.

Yet more good news is that increasingly sophisticated technology allows use of the "multiplier effect" even more than was possible twenty years ago. The multiplier effect is making others do your work for you. A good example of this technique is sending in magazine subscription cards in your target's name. Many people will ship him magazines, bill him for them, and hound him for payment in response to your initial effort of writing or stamping your target's name on a post-paid card. The Internet, as we'll see, provides opportunities to have a large-scale multiplier effect through technology. Another example is that today many people carry pagers, and this offers new opportunities to bug your target via remote control.

What This Book Will Do for You

This book will outline reasons for and methods of harassment, ways of getting revenge on those who

---

[1] Victor Santoro, *Gaslighting*, Port Townsend, WA. Loompanics Unlimited, 1994.

have wronged or harmed you and who seem to be invulnerable to the usual methods of obtaining justice. In real life, there are many people, modern-day predators, who specialize in making life miserable for others, and their victims for various reasons cannot avail themselves of the courts or other official agencies to balance the picture. This book will help level the playing field.

There are many low-life individuals you'll encounter during your lifetime, and one of the most common types is the tyrannical employer or supervisor who enjoys making life miserable for his employees. This type of person is almost invulnerable to a lawsuit, unless he's foolish enough to indulge in sexual harassment or practice clear-cut ethnic discrimination. Even if he does, you have to work through official agencies, such as the Equal Opportunity Employment Commission, or hire a lawyer to take a lawsuit through the courts. For the ordinary person, a lawsuit is often a loser, because the courts work very slowly and seem to give the benefit of every doubt to the party seeking to delay the proceedings. Remember, "justice delayed is justice denied."

What, if anything, can you do about the company spy, who will without conscience snitch you off to the boss to gain advantage for himself? Sue him? Don't hold your breath!

You can expect to encounter a number of unrelentingly obnoxious and vicious people who can make your life miserable without actually breaking the law. The employer who promises you a raise or promotion, and then goes back on his word, is a good example.

Others do break the law, but you can't do anything about it unless you can prove they did it. The person who slashes your tires in the night is such an example. You may know who he is, but unless you see him doing it, you haven't got much to tell the cops.

In other circumstances, you're helpless because of other reasons. One woman applying for employment was asked by the interviewer if she planned to have any children during the next couple of years. Knowing the law, she replied that such a question was illegal. The interviewer nodded at her, pushed the telephone in her direction, and said, "Here. Call the police."

Let's note here that revenge tactics are not for settling casual slights and insults. It's definitely overkill to practice these techniques on a rude waiter, someone who doesn't return your phone call, or a stupid store clerk. You'll encounter many of these, and they're not worth the trouble because in fact they're their own worst enemies. In short, don't be an "injustice collector." Save the big guns for those who really deserve the attention: those who have put a severe crimp in your life with malice aforethought.

Why seek revenge, when our culture implores us to be understanding and forgiving? Revenge will make you feel better, that's why! People who have been viciously victimized have one thing in common: they feel inadequate and depressed because they have been hurt. Don't feel like a victim! Revenge is a way to redress the balance! It's justified because the psychopaths who hurt people don't play by any civilized rules, and respect only the law of the jungle. If you turn the other cheek to the psychopath, he'll use the other fist! Save your understanding and sympathy for the decent people in your life. The psychopaths who purposely and maliciously hurt people deserve revenge, and this book will show you how.

We'll be discussing a wide variety of revenge tactics because real-life situations vary tremendously. Not all techniques will work against a particular individual, and you'll have to draw upon your knowledge of your target's vulnerabilities to decide which techniques will work best.

Using Your Imagination

Your most powerful weapon is between your ears. Use your knowledge of your target and his environment to make life miserable for him.

This book will also provide you with techniques for protecting yourself. It's unfortunate, but you might make an enemy or two during your life. Perhaps you'll encounter a crazy misfit who takes offense when none is intended, and you might become a target this way. That's when you'll learn how effective harassment can be. If this happens to you, just count your blessings. You might have been in a post office when a disgruntled employee started shooting up the place!

For the sake of making this book easy to read and avoiding awkward terminology and sentence construction, we're going to ignore political correctness and use the male pronoun everywhere, except where the example cites someone who is clearly female. This will avoid using terms such as "he or she" or "he/she" and make these pages easier to read. Accordingly, we'll depict the target and the revenge artist as male. For clarity, we'll even give your target a notional name: "John Smith." My apologies to all the real-life John Smiths out there who are decent people. The one we'll be discussing is a bastard who deserves everything he gets! The reader should have enough imagination to understand that these situations and techniques are not restricted to a single sex, but can apply equally to both.

Enjoy these pages, and put the information to good use if and when you're unfortunate enough to be victimized by some two-legged vermin. You'll be able to cope with them well into the millennium!

Chapter One
Revenge in Fiction

During the two decades since the appearance of the first harassment book, there has been widespread recognition of the value of these techniques. We've even seen revenge themes in popular mainstream and genre fiction.

Tom Philbin writes gritty, realistic novels about New York City police officers. *The Prosecutor,* (New York: Fawcett Gold Medal, 1991), contains several episodes of revenge by some officers against an organized crime figure. Two detectives, Piccolo and Stein, were angry at mobster Angelo Capezzi for killing one of their informers. They lamented that this mobster seemed to lead a charmed life because the Drug Enforcement Administration and the U.S. Justice Department hadn't been able to build any case against him. Deciding to strike out on their own, their first step was to procure a tanker truck from a friend who empties cesspools. This truck had a capacity of 3,000 gallons of sewage, and was full to the brim.

The two cops drove the truck to Capezzi's auto-wrecking yard used as a front for the mob. A large mobile home in front of the fenced-in yard served as an office. Inside was a guard dog. The two cops drilled a hole in the roof and began pumping in the 14 tons of sewage. After they'd finished, they anonymously telephoned the media to get publicity for their stunt.

Their success inspired them to other acts of harassment against Capezzi. Using their investigative resources, they discovered that Capezzi owned a 62-foot luxury yacht worth about a million dollars, and one night they went to the marina where it was kept. Boarding the boat, they drilled a hole in the fiberglass hull with a brace and bit, and left it to sink at its anchorage.

The two cops were both encouraged and inspired by their latest coup, and in discussing it, decided that if they were going to "break balls," they would go all the way. They began poring over the Yellow Pages, seeking companies that provided emergency services, such as plumbers. They knew that if they ordered merchandise in Capezzi's name, they'd have to provide a credit card number. Providers of emergency services, however, don't demand credit card numbers up front. They began telephoning companies that would unplug drains, clear chimneys, exterminate pests, open locks, repair heating systems, and provide other services. They also made calls to contractors, including fifteen cesspool drainage companies. Then they went to watch the action as the street began to fill with trucks. Plumbers' trucks, painters' trucks, and a Roto-Rooter truck arrived, and Capezzi's bodyguards were kept busy shooing them away. Then the pizza deliveries began, as the detectives had called about three dozen of them. Then a truck from a local TV news station pulled up.

At this point, they decided to raise the stakes, and telephoned 911, telling the dispatcher that a police officer was being attacked at that address. Within two minutes, three police cars, sirens screaming, pulled up in front and patrol officers erupted from them with guns drawn.

Seeking to escalate the situation further, the two pranksters obtained a dump truck containing the offal from a meat rendering plant. This mixture of fat, meat fragments, excrement, maggots, and other smelly, obnoxious substances made sewage smell pleasant by contrast. Planning to dump this onto Capezzi's residence, they first arranged for a diversion. They telephoned the fire department and reported a fire across the street from Capezzi's house, then drove their truck to the street behind it, where a long slope led down to the mobster's home. When the fire trucks arrived, they dumped their cargo to run downhill to engulf Capezzi's house.

These two fictional characters, limited only by the author's imagination, did far more to their target than most revenge artists are likely to do. Instead of using subtle techniques to cause their target unease, they went straight for the throat. Most of us do not have notorious organized crime figures as personal enemies. Also, most of us do not have the resources these imaginary police officers were able to command.

The Art of Breaking Glass, by Matthew Hall (New York: Warner Books, 1997), is a grimly serious novel about a man who wages a solitary campaign against selfish businessmen and corrupt politicians who are exploiting New York City for their own ends. Bill Kaiser is an urban guerrilla who uses various forms of mayhem, such as explosives and noxious chemicals, to attack those he sees as the enemies of the people of New York. In one episode, he places a bomb in a corrupt senator's computer, killing him when he turns on the power. He raids the headquarters of an alarm company and disables their computers so that when he steals a valuable painting for ransom, no alarm will go to the police. When an abusive man beats up a woman he knows, Kaiser tracks him to his home, sprays him with Mace, and ties him up. He then anesthetizes him and brands him with letters that spell "I Hit Women." He performs other acts of sabotage and terrorism, including kidnapping one developer's 5-year-old son to force compliance with his demands.

This fictional character goes far beyond what the usual revenge artist is likely to do, because although his main targets are definitely guilty, he also injures innocent people. The alarm company employees that he disables with tear gas, then ties up, have done nothing to harm him or anyone he knows.

Fiction writers can go as far as they wish, because the sky is the limit. Their characters always have enough income, and other resources, to do what they wish. The avengers' adversaries are always vulnerable in ways the central characters can easily exploit. In real life, we have to be far more circumspect because of the risk of getting caught, limited funding, and adverse circumstances.

Chapter Two
Revenge Ethics

That revenge is a righteous act has even been recognized in the mainstream press. Columnist Jerry Large, writing in the *Seattle Times* on October 19, 1997, related how his older brother had a nasty superior when he was in the Navy. His brother exacted revenge by spitting in the man's coffee when he fetched him a cup. Other sailors added more noxious substances which Large did not name.

A very important point this columnist made was that, although exacting revenge did not change the chief petty officer's behavior, it helped the men, because they "didn't feel so helpless." He goes on to explain the role of revenge in workplace injustices, the prototypical bullying scenario in which a more powerful person demeans and abuses weaker ones.

Revenge has become a definite part of our culture, with increasing numbers of people deciding that it has a place in their lives. Of course, this has antagonized the bleeding hearts and touchy-feely types, who seem always to blame the victim instead of the perpetrator. These people feel that taking revenge does more harm to the person doing it than to the target. This is spurious logic, and very unconvincing. Well, they can love their enemies if they wish, but we'll choose to hassle ours, thank you.

There are definite ethical considerations in planning revenge, and it's precisely these that place revenge using harassment techniques far above mere vandalism. A thug might cut the brake lines on his target's vehicle, or set fire to his house, without regard to the possibility of injuring or killing innocent persons. The revenge artist uses refined methods with surgical skill, to selectively cause problems for his target without indiscriminately harming innocent persons.

This is why it's important to look at the consequences of each tactic you're contemplating. Analyze each one to assess its impact upon innocent persons. A tactic that at first appears attractive because it causes no permanent harm can be very undesirable if it affects many people. For example, spraying Mace or pepper spray into your target's office appears to be a splendid way of causing him extreme discomfort, but take note of its effect on others who work there. If your effort forces the evacuation of an entire floor, or the entire building, you'll have caused a lot of grief to many innocent persons.

Let's end this chapter with a short list of "don'ts." The first and most important one is never to let your target know who you are. You don't want to set yourself up for any sort of retaliation, such as countermeasures or even a lawsuit.

Never call the fire department or the paramedics. You might feel that it would be very disrupting to have the fire engines roaring up outside his house, but also remember that while the fire engines are on that run, a real fire somewhere else may be neglected. Also, firefighters sometimes get killed on emergency runs, and you don't want that on your conscience.

Calling the paramedics also ties up a unit that might be saving a life elsewhere. A spurious call to the police may deprive a citizen who needs the cops at a critical time. These are good reasons for not involving any sort of emergency services in your campaign of harassment.

Ethics are important because you're the good guy and your target is the bad guy. Ethics are what distinguishes you from the low-life you're going to trash.

Chapter Three
Basic Preparations

The better prepared you are, the more effective your program of harassment will be. With minimal preparation, you'll be more dependent on luck, and your strikes against your target may be sporadic and not as effective as they might have been had you been better prepared. The basic fact is that we're all more dependent on luck than most of us like to admit, and not all revenge tactics work all the time against all targets. If your target is unemployed, you can't cause on-the-job problems for him. If he's unmarried, you can't provoke jealousy between him and his spouse. In such cases, you'd better have a "Plan B" as a backup. The wider the range of your preparations, the better chance you have of having something on hand for a particular target.

For modern harassment to work with sledgehammer effect, a few advance preparations will help, because last-minute efforts are not always successful. One is to collect a supply of untraceable paper. This means going to an office supply store and buying a ream (500 sheets) or more of common copy-machine paper. This comes in a sealed package, and this will allow you to handle and store it without danger of leaving fingerprints until you're ready to use it. For some of the harassment tactics outlined below, you'll need paper, and perhaps even envelopes, that cannot be traced to you because they are so commonly available across the country.

Also obtain several pairs of surgical gloves. It's unlikely that anyone will try to pick up fingerprints from pieces of paper you have handled, but there's no point in taking a chance when precautions are so simple and easy. Today, computers make it easier than ever to match fingerprints. The Automated Fingerprint Identification System (AFIS) stores millions of digitized fingerprints and running a match takes less than a minute in most cases. It used to be that manually matching fingerprints by magnifying glass was so time-consuming that police didn't even try to do so except in major cases, and then only if they had a short list of suspects. Today a fingerprint found at a crime scene or on a questioned document can be developed, digitized, and run for matches against millions of other fingerprints in minutes.

Normally, police will try to match fingerprints with their criminal fingerprint files, but we can expect them to begin running matches on everyone who was ever fingerprinted, because it's so quick and easy. Therefore, if you have ever been fingerprinted in the armed forces, on the job, in a hospital, orphanage, or almost anywhere else, your digitized prints may be in a computer somewhere, waiting to betray you. Some companies fingerprint all employees, and if your revenge is against that company or anyone connected with it, you'll be on the short list of suspects.

Another way to avoid leaving fingerprints is to coat your fingertips with a light film of Duco Cement or airplane glue. This coating is much less conspicuous than wearing gloves, and it peels off without too much trouble afterwards. Think of how you'd look wearing rubber gloves at a newsstand or in a library. This won't prevent you from leaving palm prints, but these are very hard to match, and being careful will avoid this danger, as well. If you want to take the trouble, paint your palms with a protective coating, as it's not too hard to remove.

It's even more unlikely that any law enforcement agency will try to trace you via DNA samples in your saliva, but you can forestall this remote possibility by using self-adhesive stamps if you have to mail letters during your harassment program. Likewise, do not lick envelopes to seal them. Use a wet sponge instead. This will also do if you don't happen to have self-adhesive stamps.

Another step is to establish a mail drop under another identity, so that you'll have a blind billing address not traceable to you. For those not familiar with the term, a "mail drop" is a mailing and receiving service for those who do not want to receive their mail at home or at the office. In some cases, the reasons are clear. A man might not want his wife accidentally opening an envelope containing a pornographic magazine or a package of sex toys, for example. These services are listed in the Yellow Pages as "Mail Receiving Services" and "Mail Boxes-Rental." They go under such names as "Mail N More," and "Mail Boxes Etc." You can find them in every city today, and even many small towns.

If you travel at all, you may wish to go to the expense of setting up a mail drop in another city. This is one you set up and forget, because you'll never go there again. Its main purpose is as a receptacle for your target's mail, should you decide to file a change of address card on him. If you use a real address or a non-existent street address, the U.S. Postal Service will eventually return the mail to the sender. However, you just want his mail to go far away and get lost. In the telephone tactics chapter you'll find another ingenious and malicious use for this remote mail drop.

"Blind" addresses, set up under an alias and not traceable back to you, can be important in executing a revenge plan, because doing things anonymously can widen your scope of action. Similarly, a "blind" credit card, again not traceable to you, can be very important for some revenge tactics. As you'll see, though, these come at a price.

In most cases, setting up a mail drop won't be as easy as it seems. Postal regulations require the maildrop client to show some sort of photo ID, such as a driver's license. For this purpose, "secondary" ID sources will do.

A secondary ID source is a forgery that will never stand up to official scrutiny, but will pass casual examination. A forged driver's license, for example, does not have records supporting it at the motor vehicle bureau. A police officer conducting a radio check would soon discover that there was no such person registered. However, you do not have to run a secondary ID past a police officer. You just run it past a bored clerk at a mail drop. Chances are that he'll never notice the tiny imperfections.[1]

Another source for photo ID is a lost wallet. If ever you're lucky enough to find a wallet in the street, return it to the owner, but keep the driver's license. Just slip the driver's license out of its plastic envelope and drop the wallet in the mail addressed to the person who lost it. Of course, the person in the photo must look somewhat like you for this to work. A point to watch is to avoid getting the innocent person who owns the driver's license into trouble. If you're renting a mail drop using his identity, the handwriting on the form you fill out will be yours, not his, which will clear him if there's an investigation. An extra step you can take is to obtain a new license under that name, but at another address than his.

If you have connections in the underworld, you can have one stolen to suit. A pickpocket can remove the wallet of someone who resembles you.

Another step is to set up a credit card account under a false name. The purpose is to have an untraceable

---

[1] Jack Luger, *Counterfeit I.D. Made Easy,* Port Townsend, WA: Loompanics Unlimited, 1990. p. 116.

source of funds to pay for minor expenses, such as an Internet fee.

Obviously, you don't do this where you bank. You wait for an advertisement for a secured credit card to reach you. Some banks and loan companies offer credit cards to those who have poor credit records and are such awful risks that nobody else will touch them. How do they do this? Well, they ask that the customer deposit with them a certain sum of money, and the credit limit varies from 80 to 300 percent of that amount.

Waiting for such a lead to a high-risk credit card lender can be time consuming, as this depends on your name getting on certain mailing lists. You can hurry the process by buying some of the supermarket tabloids. These tabloids tend to cater to the lower socio-economic groups and those who are not too bright, and this is evident from the nature of their advertisements. You'll find plenty of ads catering to high-risk borrowers.

When you find one, send for an application. Of course, use your mail drop as the return address. Fill out the application, and send it along with a money order for the required amount to the lender. Within a couple of weeks you should have your new credit card in the mail.

Why a money order? Obviously, you want to leave a cold trail, something that cannot lead any investigators back to you if anything goes wrong. You want the investigator's trail to end far from you, not to have this affair blow up in your face. You can buy a money order at any bank or post office without showing ID, just cash. In fact, you can even buy a money order in some convenience stores. It won't seem strange to the lender that you're paying by money order. After all, if you were financially solvent and had a checking account, you probably would not need those services.

- While you're collecting things, pick up stationery from companies and hotels you visit. Also pick up business cards. Flashing a business card is the way to get into many offices, as most receptionists will accept a business card as I.D. Keep in mind that you may need access to various companies to carry out your plans.
- You can even pick up some employment applications from various companies by making spurious applications for employment, then taking the form with you, saying that you'll fill it out at home and mail it back to them.
- On your travels, collect hotel stationery and bars of soap from hotels around the country. These might also be useful.
- Also make an attempt, if you have friends, acquaintances, or fellow employees who have personalized, printed, or embossed stationery, to pick up a few samples of this whenever you're in their homes. Also, if you lay eyes on anything with the bank account or Social Security numbers on it, make a note of it. This is far-reaching, but remember that today's "friend" might become tomorrow's enemy. You may be one of the bitter and disappointed people who discover that their spouses are cheating with their best friends. You might find that your best buddy at work is spreading malicious rumors

about you because he's after a promotion that should be yours.

- Save any old keys you have, or any old keys you find on the street. These will be very useful to you one day.
- If you know what poison ivy and poison sumac leaves look like, find a place that has them. If you don't know, look them up in a botany textbook and find out if they grow in your locale. You may even find some bushes in a city park, but more likely you'll find them in the woods. Note the location, because you may have an opportunity to use poison ivy or poison sumac with devastating effect.
- All sorts of odds and ends can serve your purposes in various eventualities. If one day you see an abandoned car, unscrew the plates. They will come in handy someday. You may have an opportunity to buy some illegal drugs. Buy a supply of them even if you're squeaky-clean yourself. The reason? Illegal drugs are terrific for "planting" inside your target's vehicle or premises. A quick call to the police can cause him endless trouble.

Timing is also important. Don't be clumsy and don't be in a hurry to get revenge. If your boss fires you unfairly one day, and his house burns down the next day, the finger of suspicion will point straight at you, even if you were totally uninvolved. Be subtle, be devious, and above all, be patient. Your target, and the police if they are investigating, will begin by seeking anyone with a motive. Chances are that you are not the only person your target has hurt. Give him time, and his suspect list will inevitably grow longer.

Taking your time also provides at least three intangible, but nonetheless real, benefits. The first is emotional. As an old Italian saying goes, "Revenge is the only dish that tastes best when eaten cold." You can derive great satisfaction from patient contemplation of what you're going to do to your target.

The second benefit is practical. If you're like most people, you plan best when you can do it calmly, not during the hot rush of emotion. Take the time to study your target and catalog his vulnerabilities, then plan the best and most efficient ways to disrupt his life. Think carefully about how the different aspects of your plan will dovetail with each other. Perhaps most important of all, you will be better able to avoid working at cross-purposes, such as instigating a series of telephone calls to him while he's away on vacation.

The third benefit is also practical. If you take your time and plan rationally, you'll devise ways of making your enemy miserable, leaving him emotionally exhausted and looking stupid to his colleagues. On the other hand, if you act on impulse and "go postal," you may produce the opposite effect. Anyone who uses violence today is automatically judged as the bad guy. The media almost always ignores what the "victim" did to provoke violent retaliation. If you commit an obvious felony and get caught at it, you and your family will suffer. You'll be the one stigmatized as the psychopath, and your enemy will receive the sympathy. A balanced approach will serve you much better.

This points up the need for maintaining appearances. You have to lull your target's suspicions and avoid escalating the conflict. One of the worst things you can do is to make threats. Even a few ill-chosen words to a fellow employee or casual acquaintance can hurt you, because this person might repeat them. Keep your intentions a deep, dark secret, and if you're forced into daily contact with your intended target, treat him cordially.

This may not be as difficult as it appears. If there has not been an open confrontation with your target, the only way he'd know you've got it in for him is if you let him know personally. You might be angry at him for spreading malicious gossip about you, but he'd never know whether the gossip had reached you unless you told him. If your target is the company spy, he might still delude himself that nobody knows he's snitching on fellow employees to the boss.

If your target is your employer or supervisor, the situation may be even more ambiguous. If he's given a promotion due you to someone else because of favoritism, he'll never know how much you resent it unless you confront him. Unless you shoot off your mouth, he might conclude that you're simply too stupid or not ambitious enough to care.

Even if your employer fires you unfairly, you can avoid letting him know how much you resent it. Today, some employers fire their employees very ignominiously, with a security guard present to escort the ex-employee to the gate because they fear workplace violence. A company large enough to have a security department has a security manager who keeps tabs on former employees for a certain length of time, to determine if they might be threats. Many security managers take the prospect of workplace violence very seriously, and question friends and associates of former employees to assess their mood.

In such a situation, the first priority is to drop off the security department's radar screen. You can do it easily by blending in with others who have received the same treatment. Most fired employees accept their fate meekly, go home, and lick their wounds, and you must appear to do the same. Don't appear upset, and above all don't express resentment or threaten the person who fires you. Keep your cool during the exit interview, and leave quietly. If you're being escorted off the premises by a security guard, you can throw in a comment such as: "Boy, am I glad my brother-in-law has a job waiting for me. I'm luckier than most of the people getting laid off."

If it seems that you have another job waiting for you, it gives the appearance that you won't be sitting home nursing a grudge. Reinforce this by staying away from your ex-employer. Don't visit the company to see old friends, because this will revive memories. Fade into the background with the assurance that others will soon be at the top of the recently fired list, and be getting more scrutiny than you.

Preparations taken long before you'll need them are a very efficient way of ensuring the success of your revenge plan. You'll be spared the frenzy of last-minute scrambling to put the elements of your plan together, and you'll be able to depend on luck helping you to some extent. Make the most of the time you have. As we'll see in great detail in the next chapter, part of your preparation will be gathering information.

Chapter Four
Information: The First Step

From the very beginning of the study of harassment techniques, it's been obvious that the more you know about your target, the better job you'll be able to do on him. Information is power, and nowhere is this principle more evident than in wrecking your target's life.

If your target is an antagonist, by definition you must already know something about him. He's a neighbor, relative, fellow employee, an employer, ex-employer, or business associate. You know where he lives and/or works, and perhaps even something about his personal life.

You should know his full name and any aliases he employs. Some people use aliases for legitimate purposes, while others are hiding something shady. A businessman, for example, with a wife and four small children may employ an alias when he dates and beds other women.

Other necessary items are your target's home and workplace addresses, telephone numbers, and e-mail address. If he has a fax, you can use this information as well.

Does your target have an immediate family, such as a wife and children? What are their ages and names? Where does his spouse work, if employed? Where do his children go to school? Does he have other relatives? Where are they?

Is your target happy in his work, or is he looking for other employment? What is the name of his supervisor?

What can you put together about his financial situation? Can you find out his bank account numbers? Does he have a brokerage account? Is he living above his apparent means?

Also important are intangibles, such as what type of person your target is. Is he politically conservative or liberal? What about his employer and fellow employees? Neighbors? Is he religious? Is he a hypocrite?

All of the above items, and more, have a place in planning what will have the greatest impact upon your target. Remember, not all targets are equally vulnerable, and not in the same ways. Your action plan has to be customized to the situation.

Trashing

"Trashing," digging into your target's wastebasket or garbage can to pick up odds and ends, has always been useful. At times, your position may provide an unusual opportunity to go trashing. If you're employed as a janitor, and one of your company executives deserves rough treatment, you can glean a lot of valuable information going through his wastebasket after hours. What's more, you have a perfect right to do so! A lesser opportunity is if you work through your lunch hour or after business hours, which may provide the opportunity to go through someone's wastebasket unobserved. Those who have never done it may be unfamiliar with the useful information that careful sifting of the trash can produce:

- Bank statements. These provide a view of his economic life, and you can glean a lot of useful information from these. A canceled check from a marina, for example, can tell you where he parks his boat. The rest is up to you.
- Business mail. You can find out all sorts of interesting details about your target's business dealings. Bank account numbers can be helpful, as can mail relating to home and auto loans. An insurance bill on a piece of property can reveal the address of a house you didn't know existed. A motor vehicle insurance bill can provide you with the makes, years, vehicle identification numbers (VIN), and models of his vehicles, which can be very useful later. Also, if he is receiving letters from companies offering him employment, you have another window of opportunity. Any letter or canceled check with his signature on it can serve as a pattern when you want to forge his signature by tracing.

- Credit slips. With these, you can obtain the name, number, and expiration date of your target's credit-card accounts, and create a lot of mischief. More about this later.
- Personal mail. This can provide leads to your target's relatives around the country.
- Prescription bottles. Who is taking prescription drugs in your target's family? The type of prescription drug can reveal the nature of the illness.
- Telephone message slips. These can also provide useful bits of information. If you'd like to know your supervisor's unlisted home telephone number, a message from his wife, telling him to call home, just might have it. Messages from other persons might also provide their unlisted numbers.

If you have close access to your target, there are other opportunities. If you can get hold of his house and car keys, you'll have a gold mine to exploit. Take them to a key shop and have the technician make copies. They'll come in very handy.

If you can get to your target's wallet, you'll have a treasure chest in your hands. Copy the numbers and expiration dates of all of his credit cards, information from his driver's license, and any other official paperwork in his wallet. You'll find uses for this information later.

If you get an opportunity to rummage through his home, bring a small portable copy machine with you if you can. You'll find this worth its weight in gold for making copies of documents you haven't got time to copy by hand. Some examples are his address book, correspondence, bank statements, and official documents.

Other Information

Word of mouth, sometimes called "gossip," can be very valuable for your purposes. If you're smart and keep your eyes and ears open, you can discover a lot that would otherwise be denied you. One obvious reason for this is that if your target is as bad a person as you think, he'll have antagonized many people, who will be eager to tell you what they think of him. These people may also have bits of hard information to pass along that you can use against your target. Remember, gossip is worthless in a court of law, but for your purposes, information received this way can point you in the right direction.

One point we'll be discussing repeatedly in this book is that your mind is your most powerful weapon. Gathering information about your target is an intellectual exercise, and the better you do it, the more opportunities you'll develop for making his life miserable.

Your target is a fellow employee who snitches to the boss to advance himself and his interests. You overhear him say that he plans to take his family and his boat to the cape for vacation. When vacation time comes, you follow him to the cape, and watch as he parks his vehicle and boat trailer after having launched the craft into the water. You then remove the drain plug from his crank case, letting all of his engine oil flow into the sand. While you're at it, disconnect the oil sensor. Your target will beach his boat, come ashore, and start up his vehicle's engine to tow his boat out of the water. That's when the fun begins. Sooner, rather than later, his engine will "freeze" for lack of lubrication. When doing this, be careful not to carry out any sabotage, such as cutting his brake lines, that would endanger his family or other innocent persons.

Another example: Your target mentions he's going to have a garage sale next weekend to get rid of surplus furniture and other odds and ends. As you already know his address, you hurry home to your trusty word processor and crank out a flier advertising his garage sale. However, you include some items he doesn't have, such as skis, tennis rackets, and other sporting goods, all at ridiculously low prices. Crank up your copy machine and print a couple of hundred fliers. Distribute these in stores and parking lots, and your target will be plagued by bargain-hunters.

You have to think and act fast when you get a chance to do your target some real damage. We'll take a closer look at taking advantage of opportunities presented by your target in a later chapter. Now let's take a look at how to use the telephone against him.

Chapter Five
Modern Telephone Techniques

Modern technology has changed the world during the last twenty years, and our telephone system has changed drastically. Technology has closed some doors and opened others. Let's take a look at what's possible these days.

Voice Changers

Certain electronic devices change the frequencies in your voice and make it less recognizable. The more sophisticated models include a built-in telephone, and controls to change your voice digitally, offering sixteen different masking levels. You can set the pitch of your reprocessed voice high or low, depending on the effect you desire.

A lower-cost model is simply a black box that plugs into your phone line, and allows you to choose up to eight different voice-altering levels. This is a portable unit, allowing use with almost any phone.

One source for these devices on-line is The Spy Store: http://www.spy-store.com/default.html.

There are also mail-order sources for voice changers. Some cities have "spy stores" in shopping malls. All carry this sort of electronic equipment, as well as various types of bugging and recording devices.

You should be aware that voice changers have their limitations. They can disguise the tone of your voice, but cannot change accents or speech patterns. If you have a thick and recognizable regional or foreign accent, it will come through. Likewise, if you characteristically employ certain phrases, such as "in other words," "now see here," and "y'know," these will remain to make your speech distinctive.

Coping With Caller ID

One basic rule in these days of Caller ID is never, never, never use your own telephone. This also means cellular phones, because cel-phones have their own unique electronic identification numbers they broadcast each time they establish a connection with a telephone "cell."

If you have an unlisted number, your number will automatically be "blocked," that is it will not show on Caller ID. However, the anonymity can also serve as a warning to anyone receiving a call from you. Another important point about Caller ID is that anonymity vanishes when you call the police. Your number, name, and address will appear on the dispatcher's screen. Depending on the Computer-Aided Dispatch (CAD) system in use, the screen will also list the names of all living at your address, previous police calls to that address, and other information.

There are still some tactics possible with telephones that do not have Caller ID. One is making "donations" in your target's name to various charities, especially those that run telethons. When you see one of these on TV, place a call and give your target's name and address. If you're challenged, hang up, because it means that they do have Caller ID. Most, however, don't bother with this, and utilize volunteers to fill in callers' names and addresses on pads.

Pay phones can serve some purposes. Let's say you've found an empty prescription vial in your target's trash. The prescription is still current. You go to a pay phone one afternoon and call the pharmacy that filled the prescription. The conversation goes like this:

You: "I'm calling to have prescription number 123456 refilled, and I need it now. I'm on my way home from work and I'll be stopping off in ten minutes."

Pharmacist: "Thank you, but we won't be able to have it that quickly. Maybe tomorrow morning, or later in the evening."

You: "What do you mean, later? Are you the same idiot I talked to last time? The one who promised me the prescription right away and when I got there nobody had even started working on it?"

Pharmacist: "You don't have to get abusive with me, and no, I am not the same person you spoke with that other time. We can't have the prescription ready for you right away. We have lots of other customers before you."

You: "Now listen, you masturbating jerk! My wife needs those pills, and she took the last one at noon. We need that right now, and I won't take no for an answer!"

Pharmacist: "Sir, I really want to help you, but name-calling won't help. If you can wait around, I'll do the best I can, but I can't promise you that they'll be ready when you get here."

You: "Now listen! I've heard enough excuses from weak-kneed jerks in my life, and you're one of the worst. You're a poor excuse for a human being, and I just don't know why an imbecile like you can hold on to his job."

See the pattern? You antagonize the people at the pharmacy where your target gets his prescriptions filled by being totally unreasonable and provocative. Every time the pharmacist tries to throw oil on troubled waters, you throw more gasoline on the fire. You can pull out all the stops here, to make sure your target's name will be remembered. Call the pharmacist all the profane names in your repertory. This will be especially antagonistic if the person who answers the phone is female. Calling her something like a "whore" or a "douche-bag" will ensure that when your target sticks his nose inside that pharmacy again, he won't be welcome.

You won't have to worry about leaving fingerprints on a pay phone when calling a pharmacy, but if you telephone any official agency, play it safe and wear gloves.

Another way to exploit pay phones is to work on your target's spouse's jealousy, if he's married. Have a female accomplice call his home when you know he won't be there, and ask for him. When the wife answers, have your accomplice hang up immediately. Don't overdo this, but a call every few weeks will work on her mind, and probably provoke a nasty confrontation. Be careful with this tactic, however, because you may be affecting an innocent person. On the other hand, if your target's wife is as guilty as he is, go full speed ahead!

If you know he's job-hunting, you can cause your target other problems by placing a few well-timed phone calls. How do you find out if he is? Well, if you know him or work with him, the information might reach you through the grapevine. Alternately, you might find a list of prospective employers in his trash. To hinder his chances of actually getting any employment he's seeking, you telephone the prospective employer a few days after your target has sent his resume or had his interview:

You: "Hello, is this the human resources department of the XYZ Company? Well, I'm John Smith's parole officer, and he's told me he applied to your company for employment."

Employer: "Yes, what's this about? He was here."

You: "Well, I just want to check his story, because he's fooled us before. You don't have any objections to employing a former drug addict, do you? I can assure you that he's been through forced withdrawal and he's clean, very clean."

Employer: "You say he'd been a drug addict?"

You: "Well, that was part of his psychosis. He had withdrawal symptoms on top of the depression, and the doctors took care of that with electroshock treatments. His memory's better now."

This is the sort of phone call that will sink his chances. Even if it doesn't work, and he finds employment, he'll no doubt be confronted by his employer, and his denials will always leave a doubt. He will also have the nagging worry regarding where the next blow will fall.

Alternatively, you can use the employment two-step. This works only if you know for sure that your target is job-hunting, and it works better if you know to which companies he's applied. First, you call one of these companies, identify yourself as your target, and speak in a very abusive manner to the personnel manager or his clerk. This ensures that hell will freeze before your target gets hired at that company. Next, you telephone your target at work or at home, impersonating a department head at that other company, and tell him he's got the job. If the target knows your voice, have a fun-loving friend make this call. Ask the target how quickly he can come to work for the new company. Once your target has given notice, he's gone. He'll have burned his bridges behind him, and he'll be unemployed.

What if you don't know to which companies he's applied? Bluff. Simply call him and state that a friend of yours who works at one of the companies to which he's applied knew that you were looking for someone with your target's qualifications, and passed his name on to you. Make a job offer, and press him to come to work for "your" company as soon as possible. If the target knows your voice, have your confederate make the call.

There are other nasty things you can do via phone if you've done your homework properly. If, while searching through your target's trash, you found a statement from a mortgage company, give the company a call and ask about your request for renegotiating the terms. When the person who takes your call states that he doesn't know anything about it, become nasty and abusive. Call him every name in the book, adding that you've lost your job and no longer can make such high payments.

If you find anything pertaining to an auto loan, do the same thing, but say that you cannot make any more payments at all! This just might get your target's car repossessed.

Likewise if you find a brochure or other paperwork suggesting that your target and his wife are going on a cruise. Call the travel agent or cruise-ship company and ask what's been done about your request for another cabin. As before, become extremely abusive, and tell the other person that there are many other travel agents or cruise lines in the world, and that you're never going to do business with them again.

Remember that any telephone call to the police results in the number and location of that telephone being displayed on the screen at the 911 console. In other words, the operator knows exactly where you are. Many modern 911 consoles employ Computer-Aided Dispatch (CAD), which also puts the history of that address on the screen. The operator will see if any police units have been dispatched to that address within the last year, or five years, depending on the system. The screen will also display the names of the people known to live at that address, and their criminal records, if any.

This is why you never, never, never call the police from your home, business, or cellular phone. However, you can call them from a pay phone in certain circumstances. Let's examine one case, in which you've seen your target drive away from his workplace on his way home.

You: "Help, 911? My name is John Smith, and my car's just been stolen. A man pointed a gun at me while I was getting into my car, took my keys, and drove off down Fuller Avenue."

The operator will ask you some questions, including the description of the man who stole your car. Of course, you give a description of your target, John Smith! The operator will also ask for the make, model, and year of your vehicle, and you already have that information either from eyeballing your target's car or from picking up an insurance bill from his trash. The insurance bill will also provide the VIN.

It doesn't take much imagination to understand the depth of John Smith's trouble. Police will be looking for a man reported to be armed and dangerous, and they won't fool around with him.

If you use your imagination, you can cause your target unbearable anxiety by playing some very tricky games with his mind. The telephone can serve you very well in this regard. If, for example, your target has children, and you know where they go to school, telephone the school and ask to speak with the principal or administrator:

You: "This is Officer Robinson of the Anytown Police Department. Little Johnny Smith's mother has been seriously injured in a traffic accident and I'm going to come over to pick him up and take him to the hospital."

Of course, you don't go to the school. You do absolutely nothing more after that single phone call. You'll have done enough. Imagine the commotion that will take place. When "Officer Robinson" doesn't appear, the school principal will be trying to contact the elder Smith, who will certainly be taken aback when he learns that his wife has been injured, and even more concerned when he learns that it was a hoax perpetrated by someone who knows about his family, and where his son attends school. If he sees this as a potential threat to his family, so much the better. You're not going to harm his family at all; you're just going to drive John Smith crazy with worry.

If you have access to your target's home, so much the better. This is where you can make Caller ID work for you. If you've managed to obtain copies of his keys, choose a day or weekend when you know your target won't be home, and let yourself in to use his phone.

Use his telephone to call a local newspaper to put his house or car up for sale. If the newspaper uses Caller ID, you're home free. Keep in mind that for your purposes, it doesn't matter if your target owns his own home. The reader doesn't know that. Just advertise a house at a price below market value to ensure a good number of callers. His phone will be ringing off the hook. If you want to add an especially nasty twist, include the sentence: "Call after 10 p.m."

You can also advertise his car for sale. This tactic allows you an extra dimension, because not only can you specify that prospective buyers call late at night, but you can have them call him at work, or come to see the car at his workplace.

You can also use Caller ID to get your target in deep trouble. From his home phone, make a series of obscene telephone calls to strangers. Simply pick numbers out of the telephone directory, and if a woman answers, begin with, "What kind of underwear do you have on?" and go on from there. You can count on a proportion of your victims having Caller ID, and having a record of your target's name and number.

The result will be complaints to the telephone company, and even to the police. The least that can happen is that the phone company will threaten to disconnect your target's service. With a little luck, and a little initiative, you can make worse happen.

Some of your female victims will be married, or live with a male, and it's a sure thing that some men will get on the line to scold or threaten the nasty caller.

When a male voice comes on, act belligerent and challenging. If the man says that he has your name on his Caller ID and will come over to punch you in the nose if you don't stop, challenge him to carry out his threat. It's a sure thing that not all of these men will be blowing hot air. Some will come over looking for a fight. Tell your angry antagonist that you'll be home waiting for him at a specific time, and give him the time you expect your target to return home.

Using the target's telephone to make threats is another option. You can combine this with other techniques. If, for example, you've been sending out résumés in his name, use his telephone to call the human resources departments of the companies involved, and act very nasty and threatening on the phone. Pull out all the stops to give the impression that your target is a dangerous psychopath. If a woman answers the phone, ask why she hasn't replied to your inquiry yet, and don't accept any excuse from her. Threaten to come over to rape her. If a man answers, make threats against him and his family. Using phrases such as "I know where you live" can be very stimulating.

It can be even more threatening and realistic if you do know where he lives. If the human resources director has an unusual name, and this name is the only one listed in the directory, chances are that that is his address. You can verify this by calling his home beforehand and asking if he is the person who works for the "XYZ Company." Then, when you telephone him at work, you recite his address to him and say that you'll be coming over to settle the score with him. You can be sure that this will bring a call to the police and an investigation.

An off beat way to generate vexing calls to your target is to make up a stamp that says: "Men seeking men phone: 123-4567." Stamp this on the margins of some dollar bills and distribute them in the seedy part of town where hustlers and other unsavory types gather. This will provoke phone calls that your target absolutely will not like, assuming he is not looking for gay action.

Another tactic you can use is to obtain a copy of the local "swingers' " publication and look for ads for massage and escort services. You'll probably find these under the major heading of "adult services." Many use answering services. Give each a call, and leave your target's telephone number.

If you're seeking revenge against a business, one way to tie up the company's telephone lines is to print stickers saying: "Telephone fantasy artists in training! Hot sex talk. Free! No 900-charges, no credit card billing. Operated by the National School of Telephone Fantasy Artists. Call 123-4567."

You can use several nasty telephone techniques if you work at the same company as your target, because Caller ID will show that your calls are coming from the same company. Let's look at several possibilities:

You know that your boss has ordered a catered lunch for a business meeting tomorrow. You telephone the supplier and ask him to deliver the lunch two hours early. Alternatively, you can change the delivery to the following day.

Your target, a fellow employee, is leaving on a business trip and has telephoned for a taxi to take him to the airport. You follow up by telephoning the cab company and canceling the trip.

Another way to play havoc with a business trip is to call and cancel all reservations. This won't cause many difficulties with hotels, but airline reservations are more problematic because many flights these days are loaded to capacity and the airline will give his seat to a "stand-by."

Another way to dislocate your target's life is workable both from a company and from a pay phone. Call the utilities supplying your target's home with water, electricity, gas, and telephone service. Do not use the old "going on vacation, would you please stop my services for a month" trick, because an earlier generation of revengers and harassers worked the hell out of it, and utilities are wise to it now. Instead, use a more subtle variant. Use your target's name and tell the clerk at the utility that you're getting divorced. You're moving out, and want to have future bills sent to you at your new address, because you'll continue to make payments. Remember the mail drop in another city you set up many months ago? This is the "new address" you give the clerk, explaining that you're going to a new job out of town. From that moment, your target's utility bills will get "lost," and sooner or later someone at each utility will begin wondering what's happening. Your target will either get dunned for past due payments, or have one or more of his utilities cut off one fine day.

Note the theme to these telephone stunts. You're not calling to order a service or goods for your target. A delivery man who shows up with a pizza can simply be sent away. However, an important delivery or service that doesn't show up on time can be very disconcerting.

Telemarketers

These are another noxious product of our modern era. These people disturb you at dinner, in the bathroom, and during other private or quiet moments you may enjoy at home, until the damned phone rings! Even more disturbing is that many are dishonest. The problem is so pervasive that the U.S. Department of Justice conducted a nationwide investigation over a period of two-and-a-half years. "Operation Double Barrel" resulted in almost 1,000 telemarketers facing criminal charges, according to U.S. Attorney General Janet Reno. The investigations involved volunteers from the American Association of Retired Persons and FBI agents from field offices around the country who allowed their telephone calls to be taped for evidence. Significantly, these successes did not signal the end of the project, because the problem is still with us.[1] There are other ways besides outright fraud in which these people are obnoxious. One is that they generate hang-up calls. Your phone rings, and when you go to pick it up, you find yourself speaking to a dead line.

---

1 Michael J. Sniffen, "Hundreds of Telemarketers Charged," Associated Press, December 18, 1998.

The reason for this is that some telemarketers use auto-dialers, computer programs that dial several phone numbers at once. Time is money to them, and they don't want to waste time waiting for a particular individual to answer. They also don't want to waste time on anyone who isn't home and therefore can't answer. Obviously, they don't mind wasting your time. This is why they deserve anything you throw at them.

Another nasty aspect to this is that many telemarketers do not show up as such on your Caller ID. This is because they use a special kind of telephone line known as an "ISDN." This is a digital telephone line that does not register on your Caller ID in the regular way. You do not get a statement on your LCD that this is a blocked or "private" call. They know that many people will not pick up the phone if the caller doesn't want to reveal who he is. Instead, the Caller ID display reads "out of area" or some such innocuous and uninformative legend. Many law enforcement agencies use the same system to mask the origin of their outgoing calls.

In theory, you can contact various telemarketing associations and request that their members not call your number. In practice, don't bet on it. The only other passive defense you have is to let your answering machine pick up all of your calls, and you get on the line only when you're satisfied that the call is legitimate, not from a salesman. The problem with this technique is that it may annoy your friends, who would have to listen to your greeting every time they called you, and might resent this. Another aspect is that it isn't very satisfying personally. A lot of us resent having to run and hide from aggressive marketers. We want to strike back in a way that hurts them.

Fortunately, there are tactics to deal with these pests, and you can use some tactics in combination with others to make both a telemarketer and another target miserable. So cheer up; a call from a telepest can be good news!

First, let's consider what to do if you already have a revenge target in mind. When the telescum phones you, order his product, but in your target's name. Alternately, you can tell the telegoon that you have no need for his product, but that your target does, and give him your target's number. However, you must avoid being cited for this, as the telefool will no doubt tell your target that you referred him. This is why, right at the outset, you must make it clear to the telejerk that he's got the right number, but the wrong party. You've just moved in, and your name is "Masters," not "Turner."

Sometimes, unless you live in a state that outlaws totally computerized calls, you'll receive a call that plays you a recorded sales pitch, then asks you to dictate your name and address at the sound of the beep. This is perfect if you want to sic the teleseller type on your target. Give your target's name, address, telephone number, and any other information you can. If you happen to have his credit card number and expiration date, you can even order the service or product for him!

Now let's progress to situations in which you don't have a target in mind, but you want to give the telemoron a hard time for having bothered you. One tactic that has worked for a long time is to greet the caller cordially, but then interrupt him to say, "There's someone at the door. Hold on while I answer it." Then leave him hanging until he loses patience and hangs up his phone. This is an excellent tactic, but diminishing in effectiveness because it's been so widespread. Your typical telecockroach today knows this trick, and hangs up immediately. This forces you to employ other tactics which, unfortunately, take up more of your time.

Wasting the telecreep's time is the objective, and you can do this by remaining on the phone with him, asking him question after question regarding his product or service. Every time he tries to close the sale, come back with another question, until you exhaust his patience or you run out of questions. Then you pretend to order the product, but offer to pay with a Sears or Mervyns' card. The odds are that the telerodent will reply that this is not valid for them, and that they accept only MasterCard or Visa. That's when you become indignant, and tell the salesman that this is the card you use, and that if it's not good enough for him, that's just too bad.

Another way to close such a conversation is to say that you're interested, but busy right now, and ask for the caller's home number. This will take him aback, and he'll find all sorts of excuses not to give you his home number. Press the issue, and you'll find that, if the conversation lasts long enough, he'll state flatly that he doesn't want to be called at home. Then you reply, "Well, neither do I!"

If you have the time, you might consider playing extended games with these pests. You might do this while watering the lawn, speaking with the caller from your portable phone. You might also do this while performing a menial task that does not require your utter concentration, such as peeling potatoes or dusting furniture. If you have a phone in your bathroom, and the telejerk phones while you're on the toilet, this will provide a few minutes' diversion while you finish your business. Have at it. Remember that these people typically are reading from a script, and you can have lots of fun interrupting them and breaking up their rhythm. One tactic for wasting the caller's time is to ask him to repeat himself. Explain that you didn't quite understand what he meant, or that you're slightly deaf. Just keep wasting his time by these requests until he gets tired of it and hangs up on you.

Another tactic is to "echo" any questions the caller asks you. If he asks if you have any children, answer, "Yes, do you?" If he ignores your question and moves on to his next question, stop him cold and admonish him that he did not answer your question.

Another delaying tactic is to ask the caller to spell his name, and his company's name. If he mentions a product name, ask him to spell that too. Ask him where the company is located, and how long it's been in business.

If you're male, and the caller is female, chuckle for a moment, grunt, then ask her what kind of underwear she is wearing. On the other hand, if you're both male, and you have the nerve to do so, ask him how long his dick is. If you're both female, a lesbian approach might disgust the caller.

Another tactic, to set his nerves on edge, is to tell the caller that the conversation is being taped for his protection. This just might be a conversation-stopper.

Fun With Pagers

Twenty years ago, few people carried pagers. Today, it seems that almost everybody has one. If you know the number of your target's pager, you can have lots of fun with it. This is especially true if your target uses his pager for business purposes, and has the number printed on his business card. He won't be able to change his pager number very conveniently, no matter what the annoyance level.

Most pagers are alphanumeric: You dial the number of his pager, and the message prompts you to enter your telephone number at the beep. This number appears in a display panel on the pager. Simply call his pager number and enter the number of a department store, liquor store, or auto-body shop. Your target will have to stop what he's doing and call the number displayed on his pager. After a few days of this treatment, your target won't know if the number that appears in his display every time his pager beeps is legitimate business, or a hoax.

You can make it even worse for him if you know the pager numbers of some of his fellow employees. Begin by dialing your target's number, and entering the telephone (not pager!) number of another employee. Then you dial that employee's pager number and enter your target's telephone number. Repeat this with several other employees, and perhaps the target's boss, as well. Soon, you'll have all of these people stopping whatever they're doing and calling your target, while receiving telephone calls from him.

We've stressed in these chapters that the more you know about your target, the more effective your campaign can be. If you know what your target's political views are, you can focus your pager campaign to provide maximum annoyance. For example, if your target is anti-abortion, you can page him with the telephone numbers of every abortion clinic in town. If he is an animal-rights type and opposes hunting and fishing, you can send him the numbers of gun stores, sporting goods shops, and fishing tackle outlets. You can even have him dialing the state game and fish department!

Likewise, if your target is a conspicuous left-winger or counter-culture character, page him with the numbers of the Republican Party, various veterans' organizations, the KKK, and any neo-Nazi groups in your area.

How vicious do you want to get? The answer depends upon your motives for revenge and how nasty a person your target is. You can pull out all the stops, limited only by your imagination, in certain circumstances. Your only limit is your imagination. For example, if you know that your target has a relative in the hospital, you can page him repeatedly to call the hospital or a doctor associated with it. If your target has had a recent death in his family, make a list of every undertaker in town and send the numbers to him on his pager.

Just the Fax

Our modern era has also seen the proliferation of fax machines, and these offer many opportunities for mischief. One way to cause your target grief with his fax machine is to generate junk fax. In this case, you can use the Green Stamps technique to have people load him down with faxes. See Chapter Nine on copy machines. This is a good example of the multiplier effect.

A simpler way of consuming his fax paper is to send him faxes yourself. For this, you need a fax machine that does not send out your name and telephone number with each fax. By law, every fax machine made must have a name and number set into it, and normally you do this when you first set up your machine. There is nothing to prevent you from putting in a false name and number, however, and you can re-program a machine you already have programmed.

Next step is to find a telephone outlet you can use, and that won't lead back to you. This can be the difficult part, and you might have to rent a motel room using your blind credit card account. Type obscenities on several sheets of paper, and tape them together. Dial your target's number when you know he won't be there to see the garbage coming in over his line, and begin sending the material. When the first sheet comes out of the bottom of the machine, tape it to the last one, to make an endless loop that will send page after page after page after page...

Chapter Six
Exploiting Unexpected Opportunities

Remember, a certain amount of your success depends on luck. To a great extent, you make your own luck, but at times you find yourself facing an opportunity to cause your target major problems, and the important point is to be able to recognize such opportunities and act quickly. You have to use whatever tool is handy, such as the telephone.

If you know that your target is going on a trip, and you have information about his credit cards, call the credit card providers from a pay phone, identify yourself as your target, and say that your pocket was picked at the airport, just before you boarded a flight. Your credit cards were in your wallet, so you ask that they be canceled. Obviously, you're not going to have the number memorized, so you just have to give your target's name, address, and possibly his Social Security number. Meanwhile, your target has left for his trip, and very quickly he'll find he can't rent a car, buy a tank of gas for his vehicle, or even buy a meal, because all of his credit cards are null and void.

If you don't have time to make the calls, or if you have access to your target's wallet for a minute, run a small magnet over the magnetic strip on the back of each card. This will erase them and render the cards useless in any automatic scanner. Keep in mind that clerks who handle credit card transactions sometimes encounter credit cards with defective strips, so they enter the number manually. That is why this method is less effective than canceling the card, but it would still cause a headache with an automatic teller machine.

If you know your target intends to fly by commercial carrier, and you have access to his carry-on luggage for a minute, you have another possibility. Even a briefcase will be enough for your purposes. If one of your preparations has been to pick up a handgun that cannot be traced to you, say bought at a garage sale, slip the gun into his carry-on bag when you have a moment alone with it. You might have to make your own luck here by being a nice guy and offering to help him carry his bags down to the car or taxi.

If you don't have a handgun, try a knife. They're illegal to have in carry-on luggage. If you don't have a knife, wrap a sex toy, such as a huge dildo, in aluminum foil, and slip it beneath some clothing. The aluminum foil will show up on the airport X-ray, and chances are your target will have to open his bag for inspection. This can be especially embarrassing if your target is female.

Another twist on this tactic is to cut out the silhouette of a handgun from several layers of aluminum foil and slip it into your target's bag to force the airport security people to open it. However, place the aluminum outline at the bottom of the suitcase. On top of it, place several extremely raunchy pornographic publications, so that security guards have to remove the porn before getting to the "gun." A visit to your local "adult" shop will show you the variety of raunchy porn publications available. These include homosexual and lesbian magazines, those devoted to animal sex, interracial sex, whipping and chains, and other byways of sex. While it's not illegal to possess these, it can be extremely embarrassing to be caught with them, especially under the scrutiny of police and other passengers.

If the foregoing seem impractical for your situation, but you still have access to your target's luggage, there are more choices for you. They're low-profile, and can't be traced back to you unless your target actually catches you in the act.

One way is to sprinkle fiberglass strands all over his clothing, especially his underwear. You can prepare for this well in advance by cutting a small piece of fiberglass cloth into very small lengths, so that the individual fibers separate, and keeping this in a plastic bag until needed.

The second way takes longer, because you must go to the place where you had previously located poison ivy or poison sumac. Using plastic gloves, collect a few of the leaves in a plastic bag, and return to where you can get your hands on your target's luggage. Rub the leaves over his underwear, mainly in the front crotch area. He will shortly have an annoying rash in a very private place.

You can pour gasoline on the flames when he returns by commenting on the higher number of herpes cases that have recently appeared. It's a good way of planting the idea in his head.

If you haven't been able to obtain either fiberglass or poison leaves, apply a small amount of liniment, such as Heet, in the crotch area of his underwear. The resulting burning sensation will make him extremely uncomfortable.

Don't be disconcerted if you've missed the chance to spoil his trip, and only catch up to him upon his return. If he returns to the office with his luggage, this provides a splendid opportunity to cause him worse and longer-lasting problems. Here's your chance to use that soap you've collected. If he's married, and his wife gets a look at his luggage, imagine how shocked she'll be if she'd thought he was going to Chicago and she finds a bar of soap with the markings of a hotel in Los Angeles. This will be hard for him to explain, although showing his wife the airline tickets and telling her the soap may have been left over from an earlier trip may solve the problem.

Now imagine how hard it will be for him to explain things to his wife if she finds a pair of women's panties in his suitcase. Picture her shock and disgust if the panties are dirty and smelly, with nasty skid marks! He may be listening to lectures about sex with unsanitary women for years, unless she divorces him.

Planting items in your target's luggage demands that you be totally unobserved. If anyone sees you near your target's bag, even for a second, your plan may well kick back in your face, and you'd better abandon it.

If your target is truly the bad person you feel he is, chances are he's come into conflict with other people. At times, you can exploit the opportunities such an incident gives you, if you act fast.

For example, if your target has just been reprimanded by his boss for a serious blunder, go to one pay phone after another that night and make many hang-up calls to the boss's home.

You can do the same if your target comes into conflict with another person whom you also feel deserves this treatment. If you get two bad guys at each others' throats, so much the better. You'll be killing two birds with one stone. You begin by making a series of hang-up calls to the person your target has antagonized. The next night, make a series of hang-up calls to your target. It won't take very long for them to conclude that one is doing this to the other, and the conflict will escalate.

If you want to throw gasoline on the fire, you may have an opportunity if one of your two targets has a daughter living away from home, and you know her number. Make a series of hang-up and heavy breathing calls to her. It won't take long for word to get back to Daddy, who will be outraged that the other is bothering his family.

Chapter Seven
Exploiting the Internet

There are several ways of exploiting the Internet to harass your target. Some of these do not even require that he be on the Internet, as we'll see.

There are various levels of security you can use to prevent your tricks from being traced back to you. Every time you get on the Net and gain access to a site, you transmit your Internet Service Provider (ISP) and other identifying information, thus leaving a trail if someone tried hard to find you. There are programs that can trace such messages. If you're merely going to post messages in your target's name on various forums to generate spam (see below), you may be able to get away with using your own computer and Internet account. Your target probably won't make much of an effort to discover who you are. He'll be mad at the spammers.

A step up from this is to use an on-line service that masks your real identity and the source of your messages.

There are "anonymizer" services that take your messages and "sterilize" them so that they cannot be traced back to you. This helps protect pedophiles and others who do not want their proclivities to be known to anyone.

The third and most secure way is to have a blind Internet account, which absolutely cannot be traced back to you, for maximum security. You'll want this if you're using your target's credit-card number to order services and merchandise, because frankly, you're committing fraud.

The way to do this is to use a portable computer with a modem, get on line using someone else's telephone line, and pay for the service with your blind credit card. It's not as difficult as it might seem to use someone else's telephone line. One way is to plug in at the office, if you can find an excuse to stay late. Another is to rent a cheap motel room, and unplug the telephone, substituting your computer's line. Of course, you pay for the room with your blind credit card.

Why not use your target's credit card number? You don't want to tip your hand, that's why! He'll see the charge on his next bill, and start wondering what Internet account is being used in his name. Unless you can "blitz" him, launching a quick series of heavy attacks before he becomes aware that he's being assaulted, don't use his credit-card number.

Vexing E-mail Messages

If you know your target's e-mail number (many have it printed on their business cards or letterheads) you can begin by sending your target an e-mail like this one:

Dear John Smith:

I just saw your e-mail number below your message on a toilet wall. Do you really do all the things you said you do? Does your wife really want to be in a threesome with a younger man? If so, please contact me.

You sign your message with your alias, and include your phony e-mail address. You'll have your target wondering how many toilet walls his name and e-mail address are adorning. Of course, writing your target's name, phone number, and e-mail address on some real toilet walls can produce some interesting results as well.

If you want to go about this seriously, print some labels on your computer. Compose a short message setting out the sort of sexual activity the writer is seeking, and put your target's e-mail address at the bottom. It's a good idea to include his telephone number, as well, to avoid shutting out those who are not on line. Stick one of these on the wall every time you go into a public toilet. If you are not alone, simply go into a booth, where you'll have privacy, and stick one on each wall.

Generating Spam

"Spam" is a flood of unsolicited mail or e-mail, sent purposefully to advertise a product, to intimidate someone, or to flood his mailbox with junk. Spam is basically electronic junk mail. "Spammers" are commercial interests that obtain e-mail addresses by scanning forums, and recording the e-mail addresses of those who post messages. There are computer programs devised especially for this. This practice is so pervasive that some Internet users simply practice "lurking": scrutinizing forums that interest them, but never posting messages because of a concern that they'll get "spammed." Others alter their e-mail addresses to foil spammers. Someone whose e-mail address reads "Smith@ix.netcom.com" will change it to "Smithnospam@ix.netcom.com" to foil spammers.

If your target has an e-mail address you can draw a flood of unsolicited advertising messages to him. Simply visit some of the raunchiest sites you can find on the Net and post innocuous messages using his e-mail address. Here's how:

First, find some very raunchy sites. Use a search engine such as Alta Vista or another listed in the next chapter to search for sites related to key words such as "sodomy," and phrases such as "sex with animals." You can also search using words such as "pedophilia," "condom," "bondage," "whipping," and various slang terms relating to sex. When you find these sites (it will be surprisingly easy.) You can begin to have fun.

You simply click on the "Post A Message" button, or one similarly worded, and leave a message in his name. Fill in his e-mail address in the space provided. The message can be something relatively mild, such as "I love sex with animals," or "Where can I find young boys for sex?" The spam collection programs will soon pick up on his e-mail address and send him e-mail ads suited for those who frequent such sexually-oriented forums.

Of course, you don't have to use sex and sex-related sites as media for revenge. Depending on how well you know your target, you might be able to select other forums that will result in irritating spam sent to him. Try some politically oriented sites or various racist-oriented sites, such as the neo-Nazis, to flood his e-mail with messages that will drive him up the wall.

Mail Bombs

This is something like spam, but you generate it yourself, preferably from a site that cannot lead back to you. You can send your target many insulting messages, or just many very long messages that take forever to download. If you've ever waited while your server doled out your messages to you, a couple of bytes at a time, you know how frustrating this can be.

The basic technique is simple. Using an ordinary e-mail program such as Microsoft Outlook, compose a message and send it to your target again, and again, and again, using the To: CC: and BCC: boxes. You can send him several dozen messages in just a couple of minutes using this technique.

You don't even have to compose a message if all you want to do is stuff his mailbox. Just forward something you've received, such as a joke, again and again.

If you have ever received photographs in your e-mail, you know how long they take to download. If one or more of those photographs do not lead to you, use them as attachments to your e-mail bombs. They'll tie up his line for many frustrating minutes while he wonders what is coming over the wire.

The best part of this is that your target must download it before he knows what it is. You cannot look at just the header of an e-mail message and decide whether or not you want to take the time to download it. You cannot see it until it's totally downloaded.

An elegant way of employing e-mail bombs uses the multiplier effect. Simply place your target's e-mail address on a mailing list, and this will generate many, many e-mails a day for him. This is very easy, as these mailing lists have automated "subscribe" functions, and all you have to do is insert the word "subscribe" in either the subject line or the message box.

There are various on-line sex clubs and bulletin boards where you can post personal messages using your blind computer and your target's name. Various newsgroups, with names such as "alt.personals," and "alt.sex.wanted," are good for posting such ads. Here is a sample of the wording you might try:

Hot Blond Guy

25-year-old man, swimmer's build and well-hung seeks older man for sex contacts. Enjoy both top and bottom, enjoy oral and Greek. E-mail: smith@xxxxx.com
Phone: (123) 456-7890

It's smart to saturate forums, newsgroups, and bulletin boards with a series of messages, trying different combinations to generate as many return calls and messages as possible. Copy other ads shamelessly, and substitute your target's e-mail and phone number. Use different sexual interests in different ads to cover as many types of people as possible.

When you do this, it's critically important that your e-mail not be traceable back to you. The reason is that you open yourself to retaliation. What happened to one electronic junk-mailer when he tangled with America Online is instructive. A Philadelphia promoter had been sending junk e-mail to a database of 850,000 clients on behalf of its 4,000 advertisers. Some of the recipients were AOL subscribers, and AOL resented having its wires flooded with unsolicited junk. This was especially irritating because, as is inevitable in mass mailings, some of the addresses become obsolete and the e-mail becomes undeliverable junk. AOL gathered all of the undeliverable junk mail and returned it to the promoter and his ISP in one big, indigestible batch.

The promoter's ISP, seeing his system flooded and one of his computer systems disabled because of the actions of one of his clients, dropped the promoter, who immediately engaged another ISP. When the flood of junk e-mail resumed, AOL did the same, but this time included previous batches of undeliverable e-mail on top of the current batch. This disabled the new ISP's computers, as well. Another ISP was deterred from providing service to the promoter.

It doesn't take a giant corporation to bounce a batch of junk e-mail back at the originator. A savvy computer user can do it, too. This is why you have to cover your bases thoroughly before playing this sort of game. You may not receive half a million pieces of e-mail at one time, but just a few hundred can disable you.

Ordering Goods for Your Target via the Internet

On-line shopping is a growing business, and one reason is the convenience it offers. If you have a computer and a modem, you can get on line with many vendors of all categories, and order both goods and services. All you need is a credit-card number. If you've managed to obtain a credit slip from your target's wastebasket, you're home free.

Generally, ordering from the Internet requires the same things as ordering via telephone: a name, a credit-card number, and an expiration date. You can obtain all of these from a credit slip from your target's trash, and never have to touch his credit card.

Flaming

The Internet has millions of web sites and discussion groups. "Bulletin boards" and "news-groups" (these do not deal in news, but opinions) are ostensibly for the purpose of discussing and exchanging views on a variety of topics, from politics to childcare, from gardening to child molesting. While many of the participants are sincere, while some others have different agendas.

One characteristic of the Internet is that it has given rise to something new: verbal sniping from behind the cloak of anonymity. This is called "flaming," and those who practice it usually do it to disrupt a discussion on a bulletin board (also known as a "forum") or to antagonize a specific party whom they dislike or with whom they disagree. Often, flamers post very profane messages, designed to insult and vex, without contributing anything to the discussion. At times, they jump in and simply begin a string of insults, totally irrelevant to the topic, just to get a rise out of others on the forum. They know which hot buttons to push to get people angry at them — angry enough to post replies.

The main feature of the flamer is anonymity. The flamer hides behind a nickname or "handle," such as

"Red" or "XYZ" or "Sharpshooter." Basically, the flamer is a coward, an emotional cripple afraid to face an antagonist directly but acting very boldly as long as those he insults cannot get at him. One way to make a flamer pull in his horns is to challenge him directly, posting a reply to him that says:

"You are a craven coward, without the guts to stand up and tell us who you are. You're a real tough guy when you can shout your insults anonymously, but you would never tell us your real name or address."

Of course, the flamer won't ever tell you who he really is because he is an utter coward, but he provides an opportunity to exploit. You don't need to know who he is. Once you find a forum that has a particularly obnoxious and antagonistic flamer who has gotten several people mad at him, you can post one of these challenges. One of the nice features of these forums is that you can use any "handle" you wish, even adopting another's. A few hours later, you get back onto the forum and reply, using the flamer's handle and listing the name and home address of your target. This may result in an angry Internet user actually going to your target's home and committing mayhem.

Actually, you have tremendous flexibility here. You can piggy-back on to an existing flamer, or you can create one yourself. Begin a "flame war" on a forum and challenge others to list their names and addresses. Of course, you list that of your target.

Exploiting or creating flame wars may not work in the way you wish. Because the Internet is worldwide, you may be antagonizing someone who lives many states away, or even in another country.

E-mail at Work

Court decisions have held that an employer has the right to scrutinize the contents of employees' computers on the job and to read their e-mail. This has resulted in employees being dismissed because they were logging on to porno sites on company time and with company equipment, and other activities. In at least one case, an employee negotiated the sale of some of his employer's confidential documents, containing proprietary information, to a competitor.

If you can gain access to your target's computer, you can play all sorts of tricks that can threaten his job. Gaining access may be easy or very difficult. If your target uses a password to log on to his computer, you'll have to find out what it is. Trying to read it over his shoulder won't usually work, because password-protection programs usually do not display the password on the screen. It appears as a series of asterisks, which doesn't give a clue as to its contents.

Some people are lazy, and keep a copy of their password taped inside their desks, or even on the cabinet of their computer terminal. This makes it simple for you. You can log on to his e-mail program and use it to send e-mail derogatory to his boss:

Hey Stan:

Did you hear what Big Shot Bottomley did this morning? He couldn't find his key to his car, so he broke the window trying to get in. What an asshole!

John Smith

Now if you don't have access to his computer terminal, or don't work in the same place he does, you can cause him problems if you have only his e-mail address. Using your blind computer, send him an e-mail reading something like this:

Dear John;

Regarding your offer to provide your company's sales figures for October, I think $1,000 is too high. I talked it over with my people and $500 is what we're prepared to pay.

Stan

Any employer who finds something like this in his employee's e-mail will have kittens, and heads will roll. The odds of this message coming to the surface are pretty good, because most company network computers are designed to place everything into memory at regular intervals precisely to prevent anything from becoming lost or deleted on purpose. Even if your target deletes this message as soon as he sees it, it's stored somewhere in the main computer's memory, and will wait there like a time bomb.

Chapter Eight
Internet Resources

With the growth of the Internet, it was inevitable that sooner or later there would be Web sites and forums dealing with revenge techniques. Today, there is an abundance of revenge sites, and home pages by individuals seeking revenge or helping others get revenge.

Let's begin by noting that the Internet is both extremely widespread and extremely volatile. There are people and groups from literally all over the world on the Net, and English seems to be taking over as the common language.

Web sites are also very volatile, which is why we'll be presenting very few Web sites in these pages, compared to the many actually on the Net. A site you find today may be gone tomorrow. One or more new sites may have sprung up overnight.

Search Engines

The first step in finding Web sites dealing with your special interest (in this case revenge) is to use a search engine. Search engines are programs accessible from your computer that can literally search the Internet for sites containing words or phrases you're seeking. Searching, however, is as much art as science. It isn't enough to type in "revenge" if you want to be thorough. You should try words such as "harassment" as well. Use your imagination. Also be prepared to sift through a lot of irrelevant junk. There are music groups that use "revenge" in their names, and other sites that use the word, yet have nothing to do with what we're discussing here.

Another problem with search engines is that many Web site operators use trickery to get your attention. They need to build up "hits," that is, people who visit their sites, to increase the fees they charge their advertisers. They do this by flooding search engines with an excessive number of key words, which have nothing to do with their sites, in order to attract hits.

An example of this took place when Britain's Princess Diana died in a car crash. There was a sudden surge of words relating to the news, such as "Diana," "car," and "crash," flooding the sites. One search engine, AltaVista, has announced that it is taking steps to correct this by filtering out sites with irrelevant or inappropriate language, but we have yet to see if this will be effective, or whether the problem will worsen. Meanwhile, be prepared to dig through a lot of crap, including all sorts of pornographic sites, when you use a search engine.

The good news about search engines is that they're relatively stable. Try these:

AltaVista — http://www.altavista.com/

AltaVista will help you find web sites, people, stock quotes, and actually more information than you can ever use. With this, like all the search engines that follow, the art is to narrow your search to the sites that interest you. AltaVista has an easy to use search limiter, so that you won't find your list cluttered with rock groups and the like.

Right on the first page, you'll see a box for the language you want to use. You'll probably want to find only English-language sites, as those in languages you don't read won't be of much use and will only clutter up your list.

Dogpile — http://www.dogpile.com

Dogpile is a sort of super search engine. This piggybacks on other search engines to search the World Wide Web for the topic or words you select. If you don't want to look up all of the other search engines, begin with Dogpile and you'll probably get more material than you can use.

Excite — http://www.excite.com

This is an all-purpose site, which provides a variety of services to the user. You can type in a word or phrase in a space at the top of the page, and the engine will list all the sites it finds relating to that word or topic. Excite also provides a lot of other information, such as stock quotes and various categories of news, on demand. One service of interest to you is the "people finder," which culls the telephone directories.

Hotbot — http://www.hotbot.com/

Hotbot allows you to search the Web for words or phrases, specifying the time period, and in whichever language you choose. In practice, you'll probably want to limit your search to English. You also have other choices, allowing you to specify pages with images, video, JavaScript, and audio, if you wish. You can design the return results within limits, specifying how many you want listed on each page, and whether you want full descriptions or just names.

An extra feature accessible through Hotbot is a special high-powered people finder, available through their "reverse lookup" search. This allows you to search for people by their address or their phone number. As with other people finders, this won't produce unlisted numbers, but on the page is an option for a fee-based searcher. At the time of writing, the fee was 50 cents per search, using public-based records.

Infoseek — http://www.infoseek.com/

This search engine allows a couple of extra functions. You can exercise "extra search precision" with a special function on Infoseek, which can save you time. This allows you to limit your search to Web sites, news, companies, and newsgroups. You can also search for persons, their telephone numbers, and their e-mail addresses.

Lycos — http://www.lycos.com/
Lycos is a simple search engine, but one which also allows searching with Hotbot. Also included is WhoWhere.com, a search engine to allow you to search for people.

Webcrawler — http://webcrawler.com/
This allows a simple search on a topic, and has buttons to push for the Yellow Pages, a people finder, and other useful functions.

Yahoo! — http://www.yahoo.com/
Yahoo begins with a simple search function, and additional buttons bring you to the Yellow Pages, and a people search. There are options available in the search, accessible by clicking on the "Options" button.

Other Web Sites

Amazon.com — http://www.amazon.com
This is an on-line bookstore that allows searching for titles on any topic, such as "revenge." Prices are very competitive, lower than those of many local bookstores, even when you add the shipping charges. This is an overall good source for revenge books, as well as many other categories and titles.

Anywho Directories — http://www.anywho.com/
This is a comprehensive people and business search engine that can obtain telephone numbers for both in-

dividuals and businesses, carry out a reverse search, find toll-free numbers, and look up web sites.

Revenge Unlimited — http://www.revengeunlimited.com/
Revenge Unlimited is a clearinghouse for revenge artists, listing various tools and techniques. There are also commercial links, which sell products and services relating to revenge. You can find books dealing with revenge for sale here, as well as programs to help you plan your revenge.

If you hate telemarketers, there is a site for you:
http://www.antitelemarketer.com/
This is the home page of a very comprehensive site that tells you everything from soup to nuts about these telepests, and how to combat them. There are links, most of which work, to other pages that provide information and tips on tactics to make life miserable for televermin.

Don't Believe Everything You Read

Once you begin reading the material listed on some of the revenge sites, you'll note a peculiarity. Some of the ideas listed are wildly speculative and not practical at all. In fact, some are blatantly impossible or extremely difficult to execute. One revenge idea on the Net begins with the phrase, "Find a liquid high explosive that does not react with water or gasoline..." This might be attainable if you're a chemist specializing in ordnance research, but for an average guy who's had only high school or college chemistry twenty years before, it's pretty unworkable.

One imaginative revenge artist posted the results of his escapade on the Internet. He advocated venting your spleen on someone you don't know, and related how he'd been inspired to begin doing this. One day he dialed a wrong number, and the other person was so rude to him that after he'd connected with the right party, he called the wrong number back and said, "You're a jackass!" and hung up immediately. Thereafter, whenever he was unhappy or angry, he'd dial this party and yell, "You're a jackass!," and hang up.

When Caller ID came to his area, he realized that this might put a crimp in his plans. He called the same party, posing as a sales agent for the telephone company, and asked him if he'd heard of Caller ID yet. The rude man said, "No," and slammed down his phone. That was all he needed to continue his harassment unhampered.

An incident in a parking lot put the whole business into sharp focus for him. One day, he was waiting for an old lady to back out of a parking space. As soon as the space was clear, a man in a sports car came shooting into the space. When our hero tried to protest that he'd been there first, the man ignored him and walked into the store. Then he saw a "For Sale" sign in the car's window, and he copied the phone number listed.

A few days later, at work, he'd just called the first jackass to shout, "You're a jackass!" at him when he noticed the paper with the second number on it. He dialed, and when the man came on the line, asked,

"Are you the one with the white Camaro for sale?" When the man said he was, he asked the address, and when it would be convenient to come see it. Then he shouted, "You're a jackass!" and hung up. Now he had two people to insult when he felt aggrieved.

Months later, the thrill had faded, and he was seeking something new to revive the pleasure of hassling these two jackasses. He called the first, and yelled, "You're a jackass!", but remained on the line. The man asked him to stop calling him, and our hero refused. The man asked him for his name, and our hero gave him the name and address of the second jackass with the white Camaro. The man replied that he was coming over to settle the score in person. Our hero dared him to do so, hung up, and called the second jackass.

He began with, "Hello, jackass." The man at the other end of the line replied, "If I find out who you are..." and our hero replied that he was coming over right away. Then he hung up, called the police, told them he was the second man, and intended to kill his gay lover as soon as he got home. Then he called a TV news station and told them there was a serious disturbance at the scene. Then he drove over to the area to watch the fun, which included six patrol cars and a TV helicopter.

This story, although entertaining, has a serious flaw. Today police have 911 consoles which include Caller ID, and it would be impossible to make the call to the police as described unless our revenger was using the target's phone. However, this doesn't mean that the story is utterly worthless as a source of inspiration. It's possible to set up a conflict between two antagonists by using pay phones, and omitting the call to the police. Alternately, you could be near the scene of the fight, and call the police as a bystander from a pay phone as soon as the fight begins. The TV news station would pick it up on its police band scanner.

Another twist you could give to the tactic is to say, "They said he has a gun," during your pay phone call to police. This guarantees a quick response from the cops.

Another parking space thief story was posted on the newsgroup "alt.revenge." One revenge artist stated that he had anticipated the need for revenge on this occasion because this had happened to him before and he had previously had a steel plate fabricated with a screw through it. The plate was curved to fit inside a boot, and the screw was sharpened to a point and pushed through the leather at the boot's toe. The man who took his parking space had been particularly offensive, giving him the middle-finger salute even though he had not even honked his horn.

He waited until the man returned and got into his car, then walked over and tapped on his window, saying that he thought the man had a leak in one of his tires. When the man got out of his car, our hero walked to the front tire and kicked it, driving the nail through the side wall. The puncture was very small, and not apparent to the driver. Then our hero walked to the right front tire, and kicked that one, subsequently progressing to the right rear and left rear tires. The driver was puzzled, and our hero said with a grin, "Maybe next time you won't steal my parking spot."

He then walked back to his car and when the parking-space thief drove off, he followed him. About a mile down the road, the thief had to stop, as all four of his tires were flat. As is customary, he had only one spare.

This story is hard to believe because the hero telling it carried out an unnecessary confrontation with the thief. If the parking space thief had had the presence of mind to write down his license plate number, our hero could have received a lot of grief over this incident.

Another fanciful account from the Internet was titled "The Vanishing Room." It allegedly took place in a boarding school, where the victim's classmates waited until he went on vacation, then covered the door to his room with drywall and paint. They did this so well that no door or doorway was visible. They also installed a light fixture on the new wall section to confuse their victim further. Upon his return, the victim went ape. He began trying to break down the section of wall to get to his room, while his buddies called security to report a madman smashing the wall with a hammer.

Another account told of a "non-destructive" prank played upon tourists. Someone who managed to gain access to their hotel room played a trick with the camera they had left behind. When the tourists got their photos back from the processor, they found a picture of two hairy pairs of buttocks. Sticking out of each asshole was the handle of one of their toothbrushes.

The net result is that you'll have to sift through a lot of material to find revenge ideas on the Internet. It's worth the effort, because searching is so easy, and separating the wheat from the chaff won't be terribly difficult if you're a fast reader. In the meantime, some of the material will provide some good laughs, if nothing else.

Chapter Nine
Copy Machines

Years ago, you had to go to a print shop or a copy shop to have flyers printed. Today, copy machines suitable for home use are very inexpensive, and you can get into the business of printing your own flyers without fear of detection. This is especially important if you're printing some really nasty flyers.

What do you print? Remember the old technique of jamming up a company's parking lot by printing spurious flyers advertising a recycling program? The flyers state that the company will pay a certain amount for bottles, cans, and old tires, and that all who wish to receive cash for their junk should bring it to the listed address on the following Sunday, fill out the coupon listing the items brought (the coupon is part of the flyer), and slip the coupon into the company's mail box.

This can work with anyone or any company that has an address and physical location. If you're mad at a certain social club, bank, or any sort of institution, you can advertise a recycling program.

This can also work for private individuals, especially if they own their own houses, and particularly if they have lawns. All it needs is a little imagination. You compose and duplicate a flyer that reads like this:

BIG FOURTH OF JULY PARTY!

John Smith is helping our veterans to celebrate the Fourth of July this year with a gala party.

Come one, come all! Free food and beer!

Come to 1234 56th Avenue at 1 p.m. to celebrate the Fourth! Bring your family and friends!

Now a Fourth of July party appears innocuous, and you might imagine that this will cause a lot of disappointment among many people, who will go home peacefully when they find out they've been the victims of a hoax. Not necessarily. Much depends on where you distribute the flyers. If you place a short stack in several biker bars, you'll attract some unsavory characters to John Smith's residence. Placing flyers on skid row will bring a bunch of drunks. If you place stacks of flyers in bars and shops frequented by members of two or more rival street gangs, your target will have a real problem on his hands.

Another use for your copy machine is to make copies of his résumé, if you can get hold of one. You may also choose to leave the "original" in one of the copy machines at work, for someone else to find. If you can't get your target's real résumé, make one up. Don't even strive for accuracy, because your point is not to find him a job, but to ease him out of his present one. Send a copy of his résumé, real or fake, to every employer in his field within 30 miles. Of course, the cover letter states that the prospective employer may call his present boss for references. Naturally, you can always help this process along with a telephone call or two.

You select a company where you know the name of the CEO or human resources director. Then telephone your target's employer, asking for his supervisor. Remember that it doesn't really matter if you speak with him or not. Just use the name of the other company's CEO, and say that you're checking references because you're considering hiring Mr. Smith. This will cause waves at Smith's workplace.

An especially nasty twist is to mail a résumé to Smith's supervisor. Smith will be unable to explain this, and the incident will stick in his boss's mind. The inevitable suspicion will be that Smith is looking for other employment, and maybe his wife sent a résumé to his present employer. One way of ensuring that Smith gets compromised by his résumé is to use a company envelope and address it to another company in the same field. However, do not put a stamp on it. The post office will return it to the company, and chances are overwhelming that someone other than

Smith will open it. However, be aware that luck may run against you. The envelope might fall into the hands of a particularly unimaginative employee who will simply stick a stamp on it and drop it into the outgoing mail.

If you've had an opportunity to go through your target's desk or his home, you may have found a letter from a company offering employment. A copy machine comes in handy here, as you'll want to make several copies and mail one to his present employer. If you find more than one such letter, copy them all, and drop them into the mail. When your target's employer sees them, he may wonder who sent them, and suspect that someone is trying to do his employee some harm, but the overriding aspect will be that one of his employees is trying to jump ship. Some bosses don't take kindly to this, and have been known to fire on the spot anyone who gives them notice.

In any event, it's common practice not to promote an employee who is known to be looking elsewhere. Whatever career your target might have been building at his present employer will come to a screeching halt. You can burn bridges ahead of him as well, by using a telephone technique. If you've found letters from other companies offering him employment, make a few phone calls on his behalf. Do not call the person who signed the letter, but his superior, and complain about the terms offered. The reason is that the person sending your target the letter may well be the one who interviewed him, and might recognize that your voice is different. When you connect with the supervisor, be as abusive as you can. Denounce the letter-writer for offering so little money, and make insulting comments about any moron who would hire such a person. Make sure that you get the supervisor so angry he slams the phone down on you. He'll surely pass the word along to his subordinate that your target is not welcome in that company.

Another way to cause your target vexation is a variant on the "Free Green Stamps" technique. Traditionally, you placed a newspaper ad offering free Green Stamps and listing your target's phone number. However, as Green Stamps are not often found any more, you should offer something else, such as "Free Internet Access" or "Free Car Wash." For extra nastiness, the ad might read: "Call after 11 p.m." Today, there's another possibility, if your target has a fax machine. You make up a flyer on your computer:

Free Car Wash

Offering **Five Free Car Washes** to the first hundred people who fill out this form and fax it in. Don't delay. Coupons are redeemable at any car wash.

Name______________________________

Address____________________________

City______________State_____Zip Code________

Telephone number____________________

Fax this form to:

John Smith & Company
(123) 456-7890

Do this today! Don't be left out!

Go to a parking lot and slip a flyer under each car's windshield wiper blades. This and the newspaper ad technique are perfect examples of using the multiplier effect, getting others to do the work for you.

If your target is a business that has done you wrong, you can cause the owner or manager grief by printing up coupons, offering an oil change for five dollars or a pair of shoes for ten, depending on the nature of the business. Alternately, you can print coupons offering ten dollars off any item in the store or any service performed. A coupon offering "Free Brake Inspection" will cause people to line up at a brake shop, and if you throw in a free tank of gas as an extra incentive, this practically guarantees that the business will be mobbed.

There's no limit to this technique. If your pet peeve is against a supermarket, print coupons offering a free turkey, ham, or any other food item. To ruin a beauty-parlor manager's day, print coupons offering free shampoos or perms to the first fifty people.

Another way to employ a copy machine to generate telephone calls to your target is to compose a flyer such as the following:

Psychology Student Seeks Volunteers

Talk Dirty to Me

I am doing a research project on varieties of obscenities and ways of expressing them in our culture. Am willing to pay volunteers who telephone me and tell me how they employ obscenities, maledictions, and just plain cussin'. Give me examples over the phone, and I'll mail you a check.

John Smith 123-4567

A nastier way of employing your copy machine is to reproduce a spurious and defamatory newspaper article about your target. A modern word processor can produce type fonts, such as Times Roman, of the sort used in newspapers. A scanner can make a half-tone copy of a photograph that you can place at the start of your purported newspaper article. The text can be like this:

Chester The Molester Sentenced

Chester Snodgrass, 36, was sentenced yesterday in Superior Court to spend the next five years in prison for sexual contact with a neighbor's 10-year-old boy. Snodgrass had been convicted of inviting the boy to his home, where he persuaded him to disrobe and pose for photographs. Then Snodgrass began fondling the boy, according to testimony, and ended up having oral sex with him. The boy, whose name is being withheld because of his age, will undergo counseling for the next two years after being traumatized by the incident.

According to police, Snodgrass is suspected of having molested other neighborhood boys, but to date none have stepped forward. Parents in the area were relieved that Snodgrass will be safely locked up for five years.

Police Captain Charles Justice was quoted as saying, "Five years is too short a sentence for a guy like this, but it's all the law allows. I think that when he comes out, he'll change his name to something like 'John Smith' and move to another city."

Once you have the text and picture together on the same page, make copies and distribute them in your target's neighborhood. Staple some to telephone poles one night, slip some under windshield wipers, and make sure a lot of people see them.

Please keep in mind that you can get sued, big-time, for circulating this sort of libelous material, so take precautions. Wear gloves at all times, and use only cheap, commonly available copy paper that you can buy in any office supply store and that can't be traced to you.

Chapter Ten
Revenge via Mail

Despite a lot of hoopla, the U.S. Postal Service hasn't changed much over the years except that its services have deteriorated further, and you can still use mail techniques to make your target's life miserable. One tried-and-true technique is to file a false change-of-address card on your target, diverting his mail to a remote part of the country. An important precaution to follow is to handle the change of address card with gloved hands, to avoid leaving any of your fingerprints on it. Remember, what you're doing is a federal offense. The postal inspectors might be having a slow day when your target complains, so they just might check it for prints.

A safer and far less detectable way of using the mail against your target is to send him a letter. This can be on any topic, but making it a personal letter from an allegedly long-forgotten friend can do the trick. A better pretext is a letter from a law firm advising him that he's inherited $10,000. The point is to place a piece of paper in his hands, one that he'll handle longer than he would a piece of junk mail. The trick is that you have rubbed the paper with a poison ivy or poison sumac leaf. Your target will perhaps rub his face, or touch his penis when he goes to the bathroom. Remember, convention is to wash the hands after going to the bathroom, not before. Your target will get a rash that will cause him aggravation and distress.

If you have some contact with your target, you can twist the knife by mentioning to him the recent upsurge in new cases of herpes or other sexually transmitted diseases. If he's married, he'll have a double worry.

Another traditional way to harass your target is to fill out subscription order cards for magazines. These are in abundance almost anywhere you go. To avoid attracting notice by pulling subscription cards out of publications at the magazine rack, go to the nearest public library. Chances are that you'll find lots of magazines there with cards still in them.

How do you avoid leaving handwriting traces? You might be worried about this, as handwriting can be matched to specific individuals, and your target might furnish the police a short list of suspects.

The solution is very simple today. Office-supply stores also sell rubber stamps, and you can order one with your target's name and address. If you don't want to do this because you might have to leave your phone number for the clerk to call when your stamp is ready, buy a do-it-yourself rubber stamp kit for $10 or

$20, and make up your own rubber stamp. These kits have letters and numbers, and a frame to hold them. This way, you avoid all risk.

Wearing gloves, you simply stamp the prepaid subscription cards with your target's name and address. A few minutes' work can give your target many hours of grief as he struggles to cancel all those magazine subscriptions. The best part about this is that you can fill out and mail subscription cards faster than he can contact the publishers to explain that it was a hoax. This is the multiplier effect working for you.

If you have to sign your target's name, trace it from a document you took from his home or wastebasket. Place the document and the card on a sheet of glass, shine a powerful light through them, and go to it!

During the Christmas season, you can add to his troubles by filling out gift-subscription cards. Send gift subscriptions to his friends, relatives, and fellow employees indiscriminately. It doesn't matter if they're inappropriate, such as sending a subscription to a golf magazine to someone who has never played the game. In fact, you can get extra mileage out of these prank gifts by sending publications designed to be offensive. The social and political climate today is very favorable to this sort of action, because many people carry chips on their shoulders and take offense very easily.

For example, if you know your target's employer's religion, send him a gift subscription to a magazine catering to another religious group. Likewise, there are publications catering to various racial groups and nationalities. There are also organizations that hate various ethnic groups, and receiving mail from one or more of these will vex your target.

You can also use this technique to cause problems between him and his neighbors. If you know that your target has had a dispute with one of his neighbors, send the neighbor a magazine that he might interpret as a slur against his religion or ethnicity.

It gets even better if someone your target knows has offbeat sexual proclivities. There are many publications by religious groups slamming various types of sexual conduct, and sending a person a subscription to one of these is guaranteed to offend!

Another way to use the mails against him is to place him under suspicion at work. Whether this works or not, and exactly how you do this, depends on the type of employer he has. Today, employers are more distrustful of their employees than ever because of growing concerns over employee theft, which can range from pocketing some pencils and stamps to making off with major company assets. Embezzlement and other white-collar scams can cost employers huge amounts of money. If you exploit an employer's suspicions properly, you can have your target living under a big gray cloud at work, especially if his employer has a professional security manager.

Professional security managers have a certain mind-set, namely that everyone is a potential suspect. They know that one of the early warning signs of a dishonest employee is the need for extra money. This can take the form of crushing personal debts resulting from medical emergencies, gambling losses, or merely a wish to live an opulent lifestyle. One security expert advises that "they should always be alert to signs of change in an individual's lifestyle, including new cars or a new home in a fancy neighborhood."[1]

You can't easily cause your target or his family medical problems, cannot move him to a new and fancy address, and if he doesn't gamble, that's another door closed to you. Fortunately, the taste for an opulent lifestyle is a very easy angle for you to work.

Gather an armful of a certain type of magazine, those catering to lifestyles of the rich and famous, such as *The Robb Report,* and upscale travel magazines. Look for ads relating to cruises and expensive overseas vacations, obviously out of your target's price range. Send away for information on these packages, using your target's name and his work address. When word spreads that Mr. Smith is looking at travel packages way out of his price range, the security officer will begin looking long and hard at Mr. Smith.

He may casually ask Mr. Smith when he plans to go on one of these cruises. Smith will perhaps reply that he knows nothing about them, and never sent for any such information. To the security officer, this will appear to be a clumsy denial, especially as more advertising packages will continue to arrive. The aura of suspicion will increase.

Here's one fool-proof, untraceable way to cause your target severe embarrassment at work. Obtain a magazine with pictures of nude men, showing their genitals prominently. Using a Polaroid camera, snap a

---

[1] Christopher Giusti and Shaun O'Hara, "Mail Center Security," *Security Management,* November 1998, p. 62.

couple of pictures of a page, cropping out all type so that it looks like an original photograph of a live person, not a printed page. You'll probably have to use a close-up lens for this, and let it go slightly out of focus to blur the halftone dot pattern that would be a clue that the photograph was from a magazine. Using your computer and word processor, type out a letter that reads somewhat like this one:

> Dear John:
>
> Thanks for answering my ad in *Homo Action*, and for enclosing your picture. You've got a nice dick, and I'd love to play with it. Here's a picture of mine, and I hope you like it as much as I enjoyed yours. When can we get together?
>
> Stan

Now generate a stamped envelope by mailing yourself an envelope with a couple of sheets of blank paper in it. Write your name and address in pencil. Write a fake return address for "Stan" in ink. When you receive it, erase your name and address, tear the envelope open, remove the blank paper, and put the spurious reply letter and the Polaroid in it. Type your target's name and home address on the envelope. Take it to work with you and slip it into your target's desk. Alternatively, drop it next to his desk. Anyone who finds this and peeks inside will get a surprise!

If you decide to slip it into your target's desk, do it one day he's away. If he has a secretary who regularly goes into his desk, it's certain to be found. If not, you can mention to a fellow employee who asks you for something that it's in your target's desk. Waiting for this to happen can be chancy, and a better plan is to drop the letter in the company parking lot.

Filing a fake income tax-return in your target's name is easier than ever. IRS Form 1040-EZ and Form 1040-A are short forms and require only a few minutes to complete. You can cause your target grief if you set it up so that it appears he is entitled to a large refund. Fraud against the IRS is a serious crime, and making application for a refund to which he is not entitled will land your target in deep doo-doo. Remember to use gloves, and have someone other than yourself sign your target's name to it, just as a precaution.

Postal regulations can even help you frame your target for the crime of defrauding the IRS. If you have access to his wallet, and can get his driver's license, you can truly rock and roll, using a combination of effective and vicious techniques to get your target into far more trouble than he can handle.

First, use a Polaroid camera to make a copy of the license. Put the copy back into your target's wallet, if you're sure he cannot connect the original's disappearance with you. Next time he has to show his license, he'll have problems if the person asking to see it is a police officer. If it's up for renewal, he'll also encounter difficulties when he presents it to the motor vehicle bureau.

Next, use the genuine license to set up a mail drop in your target's name. If you don't look enough like your target to pass for him, explain that you're a friend setting it up in his name because he recently broke his leg. Another way to handle it is to grow a moustache or beard, and use that to explain the differences in your appearance. On the other hand, if your target normally wears a lot of face fungus, you're home free. If the clerk asks, you simply say you shaved it because it was too scratchy.

With that basic preparation completed, you go about framing your target. Allow a few months to pass, so that the clerk at the mail drop will have only a fuzzy memory of your renting a mail box in your target's name. With a bit of luck, the clerk may have moved on to other employment, because frankly, mail drops are not the most generous employers in town, and many other businesses can top their salaries with ease.

You obtain a short stack of IRS Forms 1040-EZ and fill them out in your target's name. Do I have to remind you to wear gloves while handling these papers? In each case, adjust the figures so that your target receives a generous refund. Send them in to the IRS, whose clerks will soon recognize a pattern that looks like fraud. Of course, you'll have made it easy for IRS agents by using your target's real name, and a mail drop made out in his name, whose operator will have a photocopy of your target's driver's license on file.

While seeing your target tried and imprisoned for these faked crimes is too optimistic, there is no doubt he will experience a lot of grief while IRS agents investigate his case. One customary action the IRS takes while investigating fraud is to impound the suspect's assets, and they can be very far-reaching and ruthless in this. Besides seizing his personally owned assets, they are likely to confiscate his wife's house, his daughter's car, and all their bank accounts because IRS agents know from experience that fraud artists often do not keep their proceeds in their own names, but transfer them to family members exactly for the purpose of evading the law.

The Crank Letter

There are many cranks in this coun t and some are dangerous, facts that police and priv e security officers know very well. You can exploit this to make life uncomfortable for your target as he finds himself under investigation.

Entertainers regularly receive fan mail, and sprinkled among these letters are crank missives. Select an entertainer, or several, and begin sending letters "signed" by your target. If you've had the opportunity to obtain some of your target's stationery, by all means use it for this purpose. Compliment the entertainer, and go on to profess your undying love and devotion. Mail at least one a week to every entertainer on your list. Don't be afraid to be redundant. Include some sexual fantasies to make them more pungent and more likely to grab someone's attention. Sooner or later the letters will begin ringing alarm bells, even if they contain no explicit threat.

If you keep up with the entertainment business you can make your letter-writing campaign more effective. If you happen to read a news story that a certain performer has been harassed this way and has hired security guards, by all means pick this one to be the recipient of your crank letters.

Crank letters can also "piggy-back" your target onto a criminal act. When an unknown person shot out the window of Animal Protection of New Mexico, in Santa Fe, several letters relating to the incident were sent to various parties. Lisa Jennings, the animal-rights group's director, received a drawing showing cross hairs and the caption "MM was here." A local newspaper received a letter stating that "MM" stood for "Minutemen." There had been several letters preceding the shooting.[2]

Whenever there is a high-profile crime, such as a shooting, kidnapping, or attack on a controversial group or organization, a rash of crank letters and telephone calls follows. Some are from compulsive "confessors," who want to turn themselves in, and others are genuine, from persons connected with the incident or those who want to make a point. The police are forced to investigate every one.

There is an important point to watch in order to make your letter appear genuine. Police investigators often withhold certain critical details of the crime, known as "investigative keys," so that they can separate true confessions from spurious ones. They may state to the media, for example, that a window had been shot out with a certain caliber, but in reality the bullet is of a different caliber. That way, anyone

---

2 Mike Taugher, "Group Claims Santa Fe Shooting," *Albuquerque Journal,* 12 December 1998, p. C3.

claiming to have used a firearm as described in the media shows himself up as being spurious.

If you happen to know the "victim," you can obtain this inside information and use it to make your letter appear genuine. If you don't have access to inside information, take a drive or walk past the premises, and note a few details. You might write in your letter that you observed the site from behind a certain bush or tree to ensure that there was nobody else present. This is the sort of detail that will make your story more credible to police, if you choose to piggy-back on a real event.

To make your target appear to be a legitimate suspect, it's important not to point to his identity in a way that's too obvious. If you sign his name or use stationery with his name and address stamped upon it, police will most likely make a cursory investigation, ask him if he wrote the letter, and then move on to another lead when your target denies knowledge. The sort of stationery that would best point to your target is distinctive, but without his name and address. Let's say your target uses "executive size" 100 percent rag paper, or paper with a distinctive watermark that is uncommon. These will point to your target if the investigation reaches the stage where police think he is a suspect and begin making comparisons between the letters and letters known to have been written by your target.

To show how you can make this work, let's construct a hypothetical incident similar to those that have taken place in real life and examine ways you can exploit them. Let's assume that an unknown person kills a prominent doctor who performs abortions. Police say that the shooting was done with a .308 caliber Winchester rifle. You know that your target is a hunter, and has purchased a .308 rifle during the last couple of years. You decide to take a chance that the shooting actually was carried out with a .308, and that this is not a ruse by police. Here's one way your crank letter might read:

> I meted out TRUE JUSTICE to the wicked doctor who slaughters helpless babies in the American Holocaust. I shot him with no more regrets than I shoot a deer with my nice new .308 rifle. The same will happen to others who perform these criminal acts.

Note that it helps to use the right buzzwords. "American Holocaust" is a favorite phrase of anti-abortionists, and one that will get the cops' attention. Capitalizing key words and phrases, such as "TRUE JUSTICE," is a characteristic of the way cranks write letters. The reference to hunting and the new .308 rifle might set the police to checking local gun shop records for the last couple of years to compile a list of those who recently bought .308 rifles.

Other ways to drop clues pointing to your target are to mail the crank letters from close to his home, use a typewriter or computer printer similar to one he owns, and to use the same sort of stamps he does. Obviously, this highlights the need to know as much as possible about your target.

If writing letters in your target's name is impractical for one reason or another, there is another course of action open to you. If your target has shown himself to be a crank, you can write an anonymous letter to the police mentioning what you know about him, facts that they can check out and verify. Here's an example of one letter you might write in this case:

> I don't want to get involved, but I think you should know that John Smith might have had something to do with the shooting of that doctor last week. He's a member of several anti-abortion groups, and he's picketed abortion clinics here in town. He's been often heard to say that doctors who perform abortions are murderers, and should be shot. Ask anybody who knows him.

Some targets make it a little easier for you by actually being conspicuous cranks or members of marginal or counter-culture organizations. Again, let's examine a hypothetical instance. A major figure in a local civil-rights organization has often antagonized the police with constant carping about how they handle their cases. He incessantly accuses police officers of "brutality," and even "legalized murder" when a suspect dies in a shoot-out with police. If you have momentary access to his vehicle, you can plant a baggie of cocaine or a firearm in jurisdictions where they're illegal. You then have two choices: You can telephone the police from a pay phone, tipping them off to the presence of contraband in the person's vehicle. Or, as a second choice, you can leave the contraband in plain sight, then telephone the police.

If your target is likely to leave his vehicle parked for the next hour or two, the second choice is far more preferable. Acting on an anonymous tip often poses problems for police, who have to justify a search based on "probable cause." If their source is a known informer, justifying the search is a piece of cake. If the informer is truly unknown to them, probable cause is harder to establish, especially if the suspect is cognizant of the law of search and seizure.

Leaving the contraband in plain sight solves these problems. An anonymous call can send a police officer to make a quick visual inspection, and once he sees the contraband it becomes an open-and-shut case.

Let's examine another hypothetical case. This time, your target is a scout troop leader who stands accused of molesting one or more of his boy scouts. You had absolutely nothing to do with this, but you're going to take advantage of the circumstances to make his life a living hell. First, procure a short stack of homosexual-oriented pornographic picture magazines. Leave one on the seat of his car, in his mailbox, in his desk, and various other places that will point to him. Even though this might appear to be an obvious frame to a sophisticated person, given the circumstances nobody will believe that he knows nothing about the porn.

Another trick you can use against him is the old copy-machine trick to fake news articles describing him as a molester in another jurisdiction. For this, you must know where he had lived a few years before, and you make up articles describing his arrest for various molestations in that locale.

Yet another way to frame him is one you can work if you have access to another car just like his. Make fake license plates with his number on pieces of cardboard, and put them on the car. Don't worry: they won't have to pass inspection. They'll just have to look good enough in a photograph.

Your computer and digital camera will help you on this one. Unlike before, you take a photograph of your target's car.

Next, obtain some pornographic magazines catering to those who like youngsters. There are many that use youthful appearing models of legal age. Rephotograph some of the pictures, and use a photo-manipulation program, such as Adobe PhotoDeluxe, to remove the pubic hair and make the model appear much younger than he really is. At this point, a lot will depend on your skill to avoid giving the appearance of a "doctored" photograph. You insert your young model into the photograph of your target's car, and you have your incriminating picture. Now you can run off all you need on your color printer, and mail them to people who know your target.

Overdrawing His Checkbook

If you have had an opportunity to get your hands on your target's checkbook, remove a check from the bottom of the pad, so that he won't notice its absence for a week or two. You'll have read in his check register how much was in the account. Now write a check for that amount to the Internal Revenue Service, forge his signature, and put it in an envelope with an Estimated Tax Voucher, Form 1040-ES. If you don't have a voucher, use the book of reproducible forms and the copy machine at your local library to make one. Fill out the form with your target's name and his Social Security number, if you know it. If you don't know his real Social Security number, fake it. The point is to get that check deposited and the sum withdrawn from his account. Mail it to the IRS office, which always deposits such checks immediately before completing the paperwork. Eventually, the IRS will discover that the paperwork doesn't check out, but by that time your target's check will have cleared and drained his account. His checks will begin bouncing, and he won't know why until he contacts his bank. Even then getting the money back from the IRS may be problematic.

Finally, let's take another look at a problem that plagues most of us: what to do about junk mail. While it's possible to contact the Direct Marketing Association and request that your name be removed from mailing lists, it's by no means certain that it will be. Not all direct mailers are members, and those who are members are not necessarily bound to obey your wishes. That leaves only one choice: Make them pay!

For years, other revengers and I have been advocating looking through each junk mail envelope to find a BRE, Business Reply Envelope, fill it with papers, and mail it back to the company that sent you the junk mail to make them pay the return postage. This is about 1½ times the first-class rate, by the way. Hit them in the pocketbook, and it hurts.

There is now evidence that this campaign by many dedicated revengers has been successful. Recently, reply envelopes with windows began appearing. The company's address is printed on an order card that has the addressee's name and address printed on it as well. This was designed to make it more difficult to stuff a BRE with scrap paper and mail it back to the company that had sent it.

The solution to this counter-measure is simple. You just cut out the portion of the card with the address and tape it to the inside of the envelope so that the company's address shows through the window. Then stuff the envelope with sales fliers from other companies, seal it, and drop it in the mail!

One problem with this technique is that some junk mailers now print their addresses on the back of the card that has your name and address, to allow them to identify anyone who does this. This is intimidation, pure and simple, and for the talented revenger is no challenge at all. Remember your valuable copy machine? Simply make a copy of the side of the card that had the junk mailer's name and address on it, and fold it to fit inside the envelope. What do you do with the other side of this sheet of paper? Leave it blank? Not unless you're in a hurry.

You can write your own message on it, perhaps printing the word "GOTCHA" in 22-point type. Another possibility is to compose your own message, stating what you think of junk mailers, and to print this on the back of every such sheet you send. Lace it with as many obscenities as you wish (the more the better), reflecting upon the ancestries of every member of the junk mailer's family and even his employers.

If you have a heavy-duty grudge against a particular junk mailer, you have yet another option. Fill out a change of address form for that particular address and drop it into a mail box. This will send replies to a place far away, and lose the junk mailer one or more days' business until he discovers that his mail has been diverted.

This is also a technique you can use against a former employer. If you kept your eyes and ears open during your employment, you'll know what address your ex-employer uses for accounts receivable. Note that this is not necessarily the employer's street address. Some employers choose a post office box to keep checks out of the hands of employees, who might be tempted to make off with them.

Filing a change-of-address card on your ex-employer's accounts receivable will cut his cash flow quickly, and you can cause him additional aggravation by making sure those checks go where they'll never be found. A quick way of doing this without exposing yourself to any risk and without spending any money is the following:

Locate an address containing a large number of offices, preferably in another city. Today, you can easily do this by looking in the Yellow Pages for another city, or using the Internet. File a change of address card on your target company's accounts receivable address, diverting the mail to the office building you've selected. Now file another change of address card, using your target company's name at this new address, sending the mail to yet another address across the country. This doesn't make your target company's mail absolutely untraceable, but makes it very difficult to return to him, given the ponderous nature of the U.S. Postal Service's bureaucracy.

Chapter Eleven
Vehicles

As mentioned before, obtaining copies of your target's keys can be very rewarding. His car keys allow you to play all sorts of tricks against him, from the merely annoying to drastic measures that will cause him unending grief.

Let's first examine simple techniques to use if you do not have his keys. If he leaves his car unlocked, at work or at home, place a dead chicken under his car seat during the hot summer months. Anyone who has ever smelled rotting chicken knows how unpleasant this can be. If his car is locked, break a couple of eggs and drop them down the fresh air intake, just under the windshield, on his vehicle. The mess will drip down into his heater core, and with luck, his air conditioner. This will also make an awful smell.

If your target happens to be well known as a member of a group unpopular with police, such as a sexual-perverts' organization or a civil-rights group, placing an offensive bumper sticker on his rear bumper will attract the attention of any police officer who sees it. A slogan such as "Off The Pigs," although dated, will still have any cop who sees it scrutinizing the vehicle carefully for a reason to give a ticket.

If you have an opportunity to get into his car, place a baggie of illegal drugs or a "joint," a marijuana cigarette, in plain view on the seat. Watch his car, to make sure he doesn't lend the keys to an innocent person, and wait until he drives off in it. Then call the police from a pay phone, telling them that you, a public-spirited citizen, are reporting illegal activity. Of course, you refuse to give your name, saying that you "don't want to get involved." This will be convincing in many locales, as citizens do not want to be seen or known to be dealing in any way with the police, and the "don't get involved" mentality is dominant. As mentioned before, the police won't have to worry about "probable cause" if the material is in plain sight.

The result will vary with the jurisdiction. In many states, illegal drugs of any sort arouse consternation, and the police will be out to investigate ASAP. In states which mandate confiscation of any vehicle in which they find illegal drugs, your target will be in serious trouble.

There is another nasty technique you can employ if you have access to his vehicle. Look in his glove compartment, where most people keep their vehicle registration and insurance card. If you find them, you have two choices:

1. Remove one or both of them. Your target won't miss them unless he's stopped by a police officer and must produce them. In most jurisdictions, there is a fine for not having the vehicle registration and/or insurance card with the vehicle. Another way of causing him grief is to make a photocopy of his registration and insurance papers. He'll hand the copies to the officer, perhaps not realizing that they are only copies.
2. Leave both in place, but copy the name and telephone number of the insurance company. Call the insurance company, say you're "John Smith," that you've purchased less expensive insurance elsewhere, and order your policy cancelled. Ask for a refund. Try to be as obnoxious as you can, to make a lasting impression. This works well in states that have both mandatory insurance and a reporting requirement that the insurance company must notify the motor vehicle bureau if the insurance policy is discontinued for any reason.

Another nasty trick is to remove the valve stem from his spare tire. Today's tires rarely go flat, but if it happens to your target and his spare is non-functional, he'll be screwed, especially if you've removed the can of tire inflation goop he had in his trunk. In other words, this is a non-explosive time bomb. You may have to wait a long time for this trick to become effective, but remember that revenge tastes best when eaten cold. It's also nice when your target is stranded with a flat 50 miles from nowhere at three in the morning.

Similar to this is replacing your target's non-locking gas tank cap with one that locks. Naturally, you don't give him a key. If he has a locking cap, use the old toothpick-and-Super-Glue trick. This is more effective if he's about to leave on a long trip, and you glue his gas cap just after he's filled his tank. Then he'll discover his plight far from home.

Now let's assume you don't have access to the inside of his vehicle. If you can get a few minutes alone with it, change his license plates. Unscrew his plates and substitute the ones you'd removed from that abandoned car years ago. Sooner or later a police patrol will notice the old plates and stop him. He'll have no explanation, of course.

Even if you don't have plates to substitute, simply remove his plates. Any vehicle without plates will attract unwelcome attention from police.

If you have no key to his car, you might find his side window cracked open during a hot day. This allows you to drop in a joint or two. If you can't get illegal drugs, drop a condom through the crack in his window, so that it falls onto the floor where he won't immediately notice it but his wife might. It's up to you whether the condom is new or used. If you have some privacy, you could even urinate through the crack.

If you cannot get inside his car, and have only a couple of minutes and a screwdriver, pry the balancing weights off his wheel rims. If his wheels are seriously out of balance, the car will be very unpleasant to drive.

Yet another way to gimmick his wheels takes much more time. Remove each wheel bolt one by one, apply Super Glue, and screw it in again. Do this with one bolt at a time, so you won't have to jack up his car. Note that if he has applied oil to each bolt's threads to prevent jamming, you'll have to remove this oil with a rag and solvent for the Super Glue to work. While today's tires rarely go flat, if this happens to your target he'll be up the creek without a paddle. You can always help him along by letting some of the air out of his tire.

An unpleasant quickie to use is to gather some dog poop, and apply it to the underside of his door handles. Use rubber gloves or a plastic baggie to handle the excrement. Then you can either go away and use your imagination, or find a place to stake out his car and watch the fun! Bring binoculars!

Another nasty trick to pull is to have his vehicle towed. Many businesses post signs threatening to tow the vehicles of anyone who parks in their lot without transacting legitimate business. The towing service's telephone number for those who want to redeem their cars is on the sign. Call this number and request that the vehicle (give make, model, and license plate) be towed. The beauty of this is that you can even have your target's car towed from the parking lot of his apartment!

Chapter Twelve
Politically Incorrect

The rise of pressure towards "political correctness" can give you many opportunities to drop your target into a pile of social dog shit at work and at home. Many people are increasingly strident about their social and political beliefs, to the point of persecuting those who do not agree with them. You can take advantage of this fact if some of these people are your target's friends, neighbors, employer, or fellow employees.

Chances are that your target goes to work every day. This means that he spends at least forty hours a week in the company of the same people. He has to follow the corporate culture to get along on the job. If you can disturb this relationship, you can make him very uncomfortable. Let's consider a few opportunities:

Your target's workplace is very "liberal," in the sense that the boss and most of the employees are strongly in favor of the Democratic Party, social welfare plans, gun control, abortion rights, sex education in schools, animal rights, and other causes falling into the liberal category.

If you happen to work there, you can cause your target grief by casually dropping a copy of the *American Rifleman* on his desk where others will see it. You can also plant literature from anti-abortion groups, right-wing religious organizations, and similar politically incorrect materials. If you don't work there, and don't have access to his workplace under any pretext, you'll have to buy him subscriptions to the *American Rifleman*, and send for information to other conservative groups in his name and with his work address. Another prospect is to send him an e-mail at work, thanking him for his recent contribution to a right-to-life group.

Let's consider your options if your target works for a company or government department with a female chief. In such an environment, male chauvinism is taboo, and so is sexual harassment, or anything suggesting sexual harassment. Therefore, you can plant a copy of *Playboy, Hustler,* or a similar magazine on his desk, in his car, or anywhere else where it will appear that he is the reader. Alternately, you can send him subscriptions to such publications.

Because sexual harassment is such a prominent issue, it has become a hot potato. This has led to situations in which the woman can state that she feels harassed, and have her view accepted by the courts.

For example, putting up a poster depicting a bathing beauty has been construed as creating a "hostile workplace," and employers today generally do not allow this for fear of being sued. Likewise, what a woman considers unwanted attention, such as notes, letters, boxes of candy, and flowers, can result in a charge of sexual harassment. This opens many doors for you. You can begin the process by sending him subscriptions to *Playboy* and *Hustler* at work, thereby establishing him as a hard-core male chauvinist. Once his reputation is established, the rest is easier.

Send one of your target's female colleagues e-mails and boxes of candy in your target's name. Follow up by telephone calls late at night from a pay phone, if you know her number. Don't say anything at all when she answers, but just let her hear your heavy breathing.

You can exploit political incorrectness in an extreme degree if you're a student and your target is a fellow student. Some schools have anti-drug policies that go to extremes, banning all drugs, even over-the-counter remedies, on school grounds. In fact, several students have been suspended for possessing or giving another student an aspirin or other over-the-counter pills. Simply put a bottle of aspirin or antihistamine in your target's desk or locker, and make an anonymous phone call to the school administration.

If you know that your target's employer is a hard-core conservative, you employ a mirror image of the above tactics. You can send him literature from animal-rights groups, pro-choice organizations, and various other left-wing causes. Send him a few e-mails thanking him for his recent contribution to a women's liberation organization or a gay-rights group.

Conducting such a campaign may take a long time. You don't want to blitz him with a barrage of mail, magazines, or e-mails. That isn't necessary, and would be obvious overkill. Just one or two items per week will do to attract unfavorable notice in his workplace.

To alienate him from his neighbors, you can pick a time when you know that he and his family won't be home, and go to one of his neighbors asking if he knows where "John Smith" lives. Make sure to identify yourself as a member of an animal-rights group, or whatever will stir up controversy. If you are one of his neighbors, you'll have to enlist an accomplice unknown by other neighbors. This shouldn't be difficult, as this is a risk-free task.

Use your imagination to exploit opportunities. By using agile thinking, you can make your target's life miserable with practically no risk.

Chapter Thirteen
Hard-core Techniques

There are many, many techniques available for wrecking a person's life, wrecking his property, and generally making your target miserable. Some overlap into pure vandalism, but with a touch of class. We're not talking about breaking his windows or setting his home on fire. We're contemplating somewhat more subtle techniques that are potentially even more destructive because they attack his peace of mind.

On Wheels

Physical damage to his vehicle can cost your target a lot in both aggravation and money, especially if you combine this with another technique; canceling his auto insurance as explained in an earlier chapter. The simplest technique is to hit his vehicle, though this is practical only if you have an old pickup with reinforced bumpers or a vehicle you don't mind seeing damaged in some way. One low-impact method that will generate thousands of dollars in bodywork is to drive the corner of your bumper all the way along the side of his car, creating a long dent in his fenders and doors. When he sees this damage and finds out that his collision insurance has ceased to exist, he'll hit the ceiling.

Another way does not require a vehicle of your own. If you have access to his house or car, consider purloining one of his garage door openers. If you're a neighbor, you can have fun slamming his garage door down on his vehicle as he's backing out. You'll have a front row seat to watch the fun. If you don't have a convenient observation post, you'll have to consider an alternative.

One way is to stake out his house, using a camper van. A confederate drives the camper to a parking place on your target's street, locks it up, and walks away. You keep watch from within the van, until you see your target's garage door open. Once his vehicle starts emerging, slam!

At Work

If your target is a fellow student or a fellow employee, you have access to his locker, desk, or office. This is where the old Super Glue trick will cause him anguish. The beauty of this trick is that you can do it quickly, with minimal risk of detection. Put a drop of Super Glue on the end of a toothpick, slip it into the lock, and break it off. This is even more effective if you drop a fish or chicken into the drawer or locker before sealing it. If you have access to where he hangs his coat or jacket, you can use a drop of Super Glue to make any zippers inoperable.

Another way to cause serious problems for your target is to plant marijuana or another illegal drug in his locker. An anonymous phone call should do the rest. Note that this has more serious consequences than getting suspended or fired. The police will get involved, and there's a serious prospect of criminal charges.

Sticky Solutions

Super Glue is so commonly available and so inexpensive, that you can use it freely against your target. Drip a little bit into the window channels of his vehicle to fix them in position. Use Super Glue to fasten his windshield wipers to the glass. A drop on the windshield-washer nozzles will block them. If you can gain access to the inside of his car for a couple of minutes, drip Super Glue into the ignition lock and various dashboard switches to freeze them.

Super Glue can also cause him aggravation with his telephone, at work or at home. Put a drop of Super Glue on the button under the handset. Hold it in place until it sets, which should be only a minute or two, then replace the handset. Next time the phone rings, he'll pick up the handset and wonder why he doesn't hear anything, and the phone keeps ringing!

Super Glue has another nasty use. If your target owns a computer, or works with one on his job, make a "death disk" to ruin his floppy drive. There are at least two ways to work this destructive stunt. The first and simplest is if you have access to his disks. Take one, and smear a small drop of Super Glue on the disk itself. Immediately sprinkle a fine abrasive, such as 300-grit carborundum, onto the area with the glue. Blow off the excess, and rotate the magnetic disk so that the abrasive is inside the outer case. Next time he inserts that disk into his drive, he'll quickly sandpaper the head, making the drive useless.

The other way is to do the same thing to a disk you obtained from another source, and casually drop it on his desk or in his briefcase, hoping that he will put this unfamiliar disk into his drive to read it. This is less certain than gimmicking one of his disks, but it can still work.

Using Super Glue judiciously can make your target's home very inhospitable. A couple of drops will freeze his light switches, thermostats, and door locks. Squirt a few drops into his computer's drives. Drizzle a few drops onto a video cassette and insert it into his VCR. Switch the cables on his TV and VCR and lock them in place with Super Glue. Unscrew a few light bulbs and drip some Super Glue onto their threads before replacing them.

You can use the following technique if you have absolutely no access to his home or workplace. You treat the disk, and mail it to him with a note that says something like this:

Hey Johnny,
Take a look at the jokes on this disc.
R.

Using just an initial as a signature may fool him into thinking that the note and disc were sent by someone he knows with a name that begins with "R."

At Home

Salt poisons the soil in a lawn, and you can use it to do this in a spectacular manner. If your target has a house with a front lawn, he's vulnerable to this. If you can pour salt in a pattern on his lawn without being seen, you can write obscenities in his grass. They will take several days to appear as the grass dies, but once you've done it, the lawn will be very difficult to repair.

If simple obscenities seem childish to you, consider various racial and political slogans. There are many bumper sticker slogans slamming various ethnic and religious groups that you can employ, choosing the one that will be most antagonistic towards your target's neighbors. Remember, they'll be very hard to remove once engraved into your target's lawn.

Another tried-and-true stunt is to plant marijuana in your target's back garden. Marijuana is still illegal in most states, and the cops will enforce the law enthusiastically when they encounter a grower.

If the back yard also contains a pool, consider pouring quick-setting concrete into the pool's drain, to jam up the pump and pipes. This works only if the pump is off, allowing the concrete to set. Alternately, pour a gallon of used motor oil into his pool.

If you can get inside his home, bring a bag of quick-setting concrete with you. Pour some into every toilet and every sink drain. For less destructive results, use gelatin dessert which can be cleaned out without using a jackhammer. If you bring a fish or chicken with you, drop it into an inaccessible part of his heater or air conditioner ducts. A point to watch is whether your target lives alone or with others. Be discreet if he's got a family, as you don't want to hurt others. There are many other nasty tricks you can employ if you have access to his home.

Put a wax crayon in his clothes dryer. The wax will melt and stain his clothing. Another way is to empty the contents of a packet of fabric dye into the bottom of his dryer, where it will tumble with his wet clothing and mar it. Nobody carefully examines the bottom of the dryer drum before filling it with wet clothing. After the dryer cycle is finished, his clothes will all be the color of the dye you selected.

What if you don't have access to his home? Send him a shirt or other article of clothing as a gift. Before sending it, sew the contents of a dye packet into one of the hems. The chances are that he'll wash that item with other clothing, and this will produce results.

Another, more insidious trick to use if you have access to his clothes dryer is to put a piece of fiberglass cloth inside the drum. During the cycle, tiny glass fibers will break off and embed themselves in his clothing. You have to experience it yourself to believe the unbearable itch this produces, especially if his underwear is involved.

If you don't have access to his home, use the same "gift" trick as before. Send your target a shirt with strips of fiberglass cloth in the hems. Of course, leave the end of the hem open so that the cloth can work itself out during the wash cycle.

If you want to be really nasty, don't overlook the destructive power of water. If your target's house has a second floor, plug a bathroom sink drain and turn on the water. The water will overflow and trickle down the stairs, through the floors and ceiling, and saturate his furniture and carpeting. Even if your target lives in a single-story dwelling, water can ruin his property. If he's away on a trip, he'll find the entire house very soggy upon his return.

A more subtle way of using water is to refill his ice trays with lightly salted water. This will give his drinks a peculiar taste.

One old technique has even wider application today. Early harassment books advised padlocking a gate to impede access and exit. The last few decades has seen an increase in "gated communities," walled-in enclaves created in response to the fear of crime. Gated communities are accessed through a gate that rolls back when the resident slides an electronic card through a slot or punches in a series of numbers on a keypad. Outsiders call the resident they're visiting, who then presses a button to unlock the gate. The very affluent have such gates for their private residences.

The easy way to cause a problem is to obtain a heavy-duty chain or cable and a large, hefty padlock. It takes only a minute to loop the chain through the bars of the gate and close the padlock. From that moment, nobody will be entering or leaving until someone manages to remove the chain.

Removal requires heavy-duty bolt cutters to snip the chain, cable, or the padlock's hasp. Some people have bolt cutters, but few have truly hefty ones to cope with a heavy-duty chain or cable. Another way is to pick the lock. A locksmith could do this in a few seconds with a lock-picking gun, a sort of vibrator that makes the tumblers jump up and down until they fall onto the gap between the lock's cylinder and body. You can easily forestall this by filling the lock's keyway with several toothpicks coated with Super Glue. It's up to you whether you want to use this tactic only with the single-occupancy dwelling, or whether you choose to lock in all the residents of a gated community.

If you can't get inside his home, but can get to his front door, you can harass him with unwelcome spillage. Cut the neck off a large soda pop bottle and fill it almost to the brim with used motor oil, paint, urine, or other unpleasant liquid. Prop this bottle against your enemy's front door late one night, and when he opens the door the next morning, splash! If there's a chance someone else might see the bottle and warn him or move it, make a call to him from a pay phone.

What do you say to him to make him open his front door precipitously? Don't tell him there's a bomb outside, because then he'll just call the police. Just ask him if he's the person who owns the Ford Econoline van (you must know what vehicle he owns to make this work) that just got hit while parked in the street. You'd be surprised how effective this tactic can be. Even in a high-rise apartment, you can make it work by going to the lobby, ringing his bell, and when he answers on the intercom, saying, "Hey, Mr. Smith, this is Frank from downstairs and someone just hit your car." He won't puzzle too long over exactly who "Frank from downstairs" might be. He'll just open his door and head for the elevator.

There are other techniques that, while not appearing hard-core at first sight, can cause your target lots of aggravation. The old trick of pasting a label inside old books, with your target's name and address and a reward offer for returning them to the "owner," then leaving them all over town, still works. It can be especially vicious if you obtain a collection of pornographic books.

Along this line, go to your collection of old keys. If you haven't collected many, you can often find old keys in junk shops. Obtain some key rings and key tags. Write or stamp your target's name and phone number on each tag and add "$10 Reward" to each label. Scatter these in various public places, and rest assured that your target will be receiving many telephone calls in the immediate future.

A nasty trick, if your target is female, is to spread a sheet of plastic wrap across the porcelain bowl of her toilet. Next time she sits down to pee, the overflow will be a disconcerting surprise!

Another technique works wonderfully if you don't have access to the inside of your target's home, but can get at his cable box or utility meters. Most of these have seals to prevent tampering by people who would like to turn back their counters to avoid paying what they owe. Simply break the seal and turn back the counter a few months in a row. With a cable box, break the seal and mess with the wires inside. Nobody will believe your target's denials after this happens more than once. He'll end up with his utilities cut off, and no chance of getting them turned on again!

If your target smokes, get a rubber band and chop it into small slices. Use a toothpick to push a piece of rubber deep inside a cigar or cigarette. Don't gimmick all in the pack. Just a few will be enough. If your target smokes a pipe, it's easier yet. Just sprinkle some rubber confetti into his pipe tobacco and mix well.

Chapter Fourteen
Protecting Yourself From Revenge

From what you've learned so far, you can easily infer that you might want to take precautions to make yourself less vulnerable if anyone wants revenge against you. Please note that vulnerability is relative. You cannot make yourself totally invulnerable unless you leave town, abandon your job, friends, and family, and hole up in a remote cave. However, you can greatly reduce your risk, and make life harder for anyone wanting to get revenge against you.

The basic principle is not to display behavior that would provoke people into wanting revenge against you. Don't be casually inconsiderate of other people, especially strangers. Granted, some people take offense at almost anything, but there are some types of high-profile behavior that will get a normal person's blood boiling and attract unnecessary attention from total strangers. If you offend someone you know, you have a chance of stopping his revenge, or at least retaliating. If you offend someone you never even see, you're totally vulnerable and he is immune to your retaliation.

Stealing someone's parking space is one such high-profile behavior. If you suddenly cut in and occupy a parking space someone else has been waiting for, you're very, very foolish if you walk away and leave your car at his mercy. The other person can do almost anything he wants, and you won't even be on the scene to stop or report him.

Another very stupid type of parking lot behavior is to slant your vehicle to occupy two parking spaces. Some people with new and/or very expensive vehicles do this so that nobody can park alongside them and hit their precious doors. However, this irritates some people, who view it as selfish and irresponsible behavior, so they run a key down the length of the offending vehicle as they walk by it. I have known at least two people who carried one of the old fashioned can openers known as a "church key" in their cars for exactly this purpose. Whenever they saw a car parked across two spaces, they'd scratch the whole length of one side with the point of the church key.

The lesson is clear: Don't act like an asshole.

One important precaution, effective against both harassment and white-collar crime, is to obtain and use a shredder. Twenty years ago, these were expensive and not commonly available. Today, they're even being sold by mail-order. You can buy a good-quality shredder for well under $100, and use it to shred all sensitive papers. This means bank statements, canceled checks, credit-card statements and slips, and other documents that might provide a harasser with information he could use.

Most shredders cut the paper into strips, which is secure enough for most needs. For extra security, burn your shredded paper. If you have a fireplace, this will be easy, at least during cold weather when shredded paper makes a good fire starter. If you don't have a fireplace, you might consider buying a cross-cut shredder, which is more expensive but more secure. This not only cuts your sensitive papers into strips, but it cuts the strips into small flakes, like confetti, making the papers much harder to re-assemble and read.

One day when you have nothing else to do, go through your garbage can as if it belonged to someone you wanted to harass, to see what a curious person might find out about you. This may be an eye-opener for you, and you'll never look at your discards in the same way again. Remember that every letter, every envelope, every prescription drug vial you discard tells something about you, something that an enemy might use against you.

There is a simple precaution that makes it impossible to divert your mail: Use a mail drop. The U.S. Postal Service delivers the mail in bulk to the mail drop operator, who might have dozens or hundreds of mail boxes in his shop, and it's his responsibility to sort out the mail he receives. The post office will not go through his mail to cull out mail addressed to a particular individual. Note, however, that there is a drawback to this. If you relocate, you won't be able to have your mail forwarded to you by filing a change-of-address card with the post office. You'll have to pay the mail drop operator to sort and forward your mail to your new address, until you've notified all of your correspondents that you have a new address.

Another precaution is to practice personal security at all times. For example, always keep your keys on your person. Never leave them in your desk. Also, always lock your car. An unlocked car in your carport is open to anyone who happens to walk past, and anyone with a purpose in mind can play nasty games with you. Even something basically stupid, such as placing a dead chicken under your car seat during the hot season can be very annoying to you as you work to clean out the intense and pervasive stink.

Give your car the once-over whenever you park it outside and away from home. At work, or in a shopping mall, look for signs of forced entry before you even touch your car. This is a sensible precaution even if nobody is trying to "get" you, as car burglars abound.

Look inside your car before you get in. Check to see that no unfamiliar packages are on the seats, and that nobody is waiting inside to attack you. Again, this is a routine anti-crime measure, necessary in many high-risk cities in our fair land.

The new millennium will contain many surprises for most of us. There will be increasing need for using revenge tactics, and increasing need to practice self-protection. In our high-tension society, the old rules hardly mean anything anymore, and you'll have to keep mentally alert for your survival and your comfort. Good luck!

Chapter Fifteen
For Further Reading

Gaslighting: How To Drive Your Enemies Crazy, Victor Santoro, (Loompanics Unlimited, 1994).

This ground-breaking work will teach you psychological techniques to sabotage your target's mental well-being and destroy his self-confidence. At the end, your target will be sitting there mumbling to himself and scratching his lobotomy scar.

How To Use Mail Drops For Profit, Privacy, and Self-Protection, (2nd Edition), Jack Luger, (Loompanics Unlimited, 1996).

This revised and expanded volume is the bible of mail-drop use and provides more than you need to know for the revenge use of mail drops. You'll learn techniques to avoid being traced through the mail or by telephone subterfuges, and to protect yourself.

Take No Prisoners: Destroying Enemies With Dirty and Malicious Tricks, Mack Nasty (Loompanics Unlimited, 1990).

This book is the manual for industrial-strength harassment and heavy-duty destruction. The tactics laid out in this manual are for when you want to pull out all the stops.

Videos

Get Even: The Video of Dirty Tricks, (Paladin Press, 1990).

This is a dramatization of various ways in which people can get revenge against others, though the emphasis is on the humorous aspects, to entertain the viewer. However, the serious student of revenge and harassment can learn some valuable lessons from watching this video, as well as have a few good laughs.

How to Get Revenge, i-spy Videos:

This revenge video is available on the Internet at http://www.ispyvideos.com/revenge.html, as designed for entertainment.

There is not as much information packed into these videos as there is in these books. If you're a serious student of revenge tactics, you'll get a bigger bang for your buck from a book. If you want to watch a good comedy, the video is the better choice.

YOU WILL ALSO WANT TO READ:

- ❑ **19193 GASLIGHTING, How to Drive Your Enemies Crazy,** ***by Victor Santoro.*** Gaslighting means to drive someone crazy. This book shows you how to destroy your target's confidence, self-esteem and reputation. Through a series of small incidents, your target gets progressively more confused, until he's reduced to a shapeless mass of shivering, quivering jelly. It will show you how to cause disorientation, get your target off balance and build up his paranoia! *Sold for informational and entertainment purposes only. 1994, 5 x 7, 116 pp, soft cover.* **$14.95.**

- ❑ **19169 TAKE NO PRISONERS, Destroying Enemies With Dirty and Malicious Tricks,** ***by Mack Nasty.*** Mack Nasty doesn't believe in holding a grudge. He believes in swift, sure and devastating retribution. In this book, Mack reveals the most deliciously despicable revenge techniques ever conceived. How to destroy your enemy's house or car. How to get someone arrested for drug trafficking, kiddie porn, firearms violations, or product tampering. *Sold for informational and entertainment purposes only. 1990, 5½ x 8½, 118 pp, soft cover.* **$12.95.**

- ❑ **19209 OUT OF BUSINESS, Force a Company, Business, or Store to Close Its Doors... for Good!,** ***by Dennis Fiery.*** When filing a formal complaint, asking for your money back, and engaging in healthy competition just don't do the trick, you need to take serious action. This book arms you with 101 ways to derail, deflate and destroy your target business. And if you want to protect your own business, this book is the best insurance policy you'll ever buy. Don't get mad. Don't get even. Get revenge. *Sold for informational and entertainment purposes only.* ***1999, 5½ x 8½, 298 pp, soft cover.*** **$17.95.**

YOU WILL ALSO WANT TO READ:

- ❑ **19106 POISON PEN LETTERS,** ***by Keith Wade*****.** A complete guide to getting revenge through the mail. If you've had problems with people or organizations that seem too big to fight back against, this book is for you. It covers individuals, corporations and even government agencies. Includes nearly 100 letters, along with tips on stationery, mailing, and how to keep from getting caught. *Sold for informational and entertainment purposes only. 1984, 5½ x 8½, 103 pp, soft cover.* **$12.95.**

- ❑ **19146 YOUR REVENGE IS IN THE MAIL,** ***by Keith Wade*****.** There are a lot of jerks in the world who need to be taught a lesson. The problem is, how to get them without causing yourself a lot of trouble? The answer is in this book. More than 60 letters you can copy and use to get even. *Sold for informational purposes. 1988, 5½ x 8½, 160 pp, soft cover.* **$12.95.**

- ❑ **40075 SNITCH, A Handbook for Informers,** ***by Jack Luger*****.** Many government and private organizations pay quick cash for the right information. This book will tell you how to gather and sell valuable information. You will learn how to snitch and collect completely anonymously. You will learn how crooks negotiate their way out of prison sentences, how cops treat informers and how to keep from being finked-out yourself. The dirt you dig up could be paydirt. *1991, 5½ x 8½, 149 pp, glossary, index, soft cover.* **$16.95.**

- ❑ **49021 FRAUDS, RIP-OFFS AND CON GAMES,** ***by Victor Santoro*****.** A startling and often humorous look at the wolves who are after your skin. Some of the fascinating scams covered include: The Dirty White Collar; Securities Swindles; The "Terrible Williamsons"; The Gypsies; Credit Card Cons & Catches; "Financial Planners"; Selling Counterfeit Ideas; Fraud Salad: An Assortment of Con Games. *1988, 5½ x 8½, 188 pp, soft cover.* **$13.95.**

YOU WILL ALSO WANT TO READ:

- ❑ **40089 HOW TO SCREW THE POST OFFICE,** ***by Mr. Unzip.*** *The Post Office!* Everybody complains about it, but nobody does anything about it — until *now*, that it. *Now* Mr. Unzip reveals lots of ways you can send First Class mail for less — sometimes even *free!* Several techniques are illustrated with actual examples of how the author saved money on First Class postage. A hilarious commentary on the largest monopoly of our time, written in the form of a how-to-do-it-manual. *Sold for entertainment purposes. 2000, 5½ x 8½, 72 pp, illustrated, soft cover.* **$8.00.**

- ❑ **40090 BEATING THE CHECK, How to Eat Out Without Paying,** ***by Mick Shaw.*** Pissed-off restaurant worker Mick Shaw lets fly at the restaurant industry in this heart-felt manual, and reveals all the techniques for ***Beating the Check*** he has learned in his years of low-paying wage slavery. This book will greatly reduce your food costs — plus, it's fun, and you will have great stories to tell! So take a tip from Mick Shaw and devour this book today. *Sold for entertainment purposes only. 2000, 5½ x 8½, 72 pp, soft cover.* **$8.00.**

- ❑ **40079 HOW TO STEAL FOOD FROM THE SUPERMARKET,** ***by J. Andrew Anderson***. Written by a supermarket security guard, this book will give your budget a boost! Learn all the ins and outs of shoplifting success, including: do-it-yourself markdowns; scamming scanner; how to dress for success; defeating store security; and much more, including the one mistake that trips up most shoplifters and the one item you must bring shoplifting with your. *This offer is not available in stores. Sold for entertainment purposes only. 1993, 5½ x 8½, 63 pp, soft cover.* **$10.00.**

YOU WILL ALSO WANT TO READ:

❑ **61163 IDENTITY THEFT, The Cybercrime of the Millennium, by John Q. Newman.** Your most valuable possession is what make you *you* — your identity. What would happen if someone stole it? Each year, more than 500,000 Americans fall victim to identity theft, and that number is rising. In this comprehensive book, you will learn: how thieves use computer networks and other information sources to adopt, use, and subsequently ravage the identities of unsuspecting victims; what you can do to protect yourself from identity theft, and how to fight back effectively if you are one of the unlucky victims. *1999, 5½ x 8½, 106 pp, soft cover.* **$12.00.**

❑ **88173 DON'T LET THEM PSYCH YOU OUT!, *by George Zgourides, Psy.D.*** This is a great book on "psychological self-defense." It gives you practical tools you can use to deal with the difficult people in your life: bosses, co-workers, relatives, spouses, bureaucrats, and salespeople — people who try to psych you out! Learn how to handle stressful situations: arguments, ambushes, and showdowns without losing your dignity or losing your cool. It won't make the conflicts go away, but it will give you the skills you need. *1993, 5½ x 8½, 198 pp, charts, glossary, soft cover.* **$15.95.**

❑ **40084 HOW TO SNEAK INTO THE MOVIES, *by Dan Zamudio.*** Why let Hollywood bigwigs, bad actors, and cowardly studio executives rip you off? The author has worked in several movie theaters and reveals all his tricks of sneaking into the movies, including the four basic ways to get into the movies free. Highlighted with true tales of sneaking into some of America's great movies palaces. If you are tired of being milked for box office duds, then lower your cost of moving-going — and your risk of getting caught — by learning exactly ***How to Sneak into the Movies!*** *1995, 5½ x 8½, 64 pp, soft cover.* **$8.00.**